新东方 XDF.CN

MW01699928

Master IELTS 4

IELTS SUPERIOR SPEAKING

IELTS 9分口语

编著/Patrick Hafenstein

西安交通大学出版社
XI'AN JIAOTONG UNIVERSITY PRESS

图书在版编目(CIP)数据

IELTS 9 分口语 / (澳) 哈芬斯蒂恩 (Hafenstein, P.) 编著. —2 版. —西安:西安交通大学出版社, 2012 (2013.12 重印)

ISBN 978-7-5605-4411-3

Ⅰ. ①I… Ⅱ. ①哈… Ⅲ. ①IELTS—口语—自学参考资料 Ⅳ. ①H319.9

中国版本图书馆 CIP 数据核字 (2012) 第 123748 号

陕版出图字:25-2008-036 号

书　　名	IELTS 9 分口语
编 著 者	(澳) Patrick Hafenstein
责任编辑	黄科丰　张　茜
封面设计	大愚设计
出版发行	西安交通大学出版社
地　　址	西安市兴庆南路 10 号(邮编:710049)
电　　话	(010)62605588　62605019(发行部)　(029)82668315(总编室)
读者信箱	bj62605588@163.com
印　　刷	北京慧美印刷有限公司
字　　数	243 千
开　　本	787mm×1092mm　1/16
印　　张	17.5
版　　次	2013 年 12 月第 1 版第 3 次印刷
书　　号	ISBN 978-7-5605-4411-3/H・1386
定　　价	40.00 元

CONTENTS

Master IELTS 4
IELTS SUPERIOR SPEAKING

CONTENTS

CONTENTS

CONTENTS

Foreword

IELTS Superior Speaking has been specifically designed for IELTS candidates whose first language is Chinese. The aim of this IELTS speaking book is threefold.
本书是专为母语为中文的 IELTS 考生设计的口语学习用书，其主要目的如下：

Firstly, to help you beat the test in a timely manner so that you can get the IELTS score that you require and more importantly make your conditional offer unconditional for the university of your choice.
第一，帮助考生在有限的时间内取得所需要的 IELTS 成绩；另外还希望能帮助拿到有条件入学许可的学生，转为取得无条件入学许可。

Secondly, to build your confidence for the section of the IELTS that most students find the most daunting and nerve-racking. By giving you the inside knowledge of the test and the strategies you can be sure that you will be able to express yourself fluently, coherently, clearly, naturally, accurately, appropriately and in a sophisticated manner.
第二，帮助考生在最担心的口语测试部分建立信心。本书提供 IELTS 测试相关信息以及准备口试的方法、技巧与策略，帮助考生说出一口自然流利的英语，并学会组织意见，清楚地表达自己的想法。

Lastly, to equip you with the speaking skills needed to not just survive in an English speaking country but also impress in an academic environment.
最后，让你的英文能力足够应付生活上以及学术领域上的需求。

There is no time like the present so stop making excuses and putting off until tomorrow what can be done today. The most important thing to remember is that you have chosen to venture forth to new heights in your life filled with greater opportunities and promises, so now is the time to get off on the right foot and take a step in the right direction.
现在就开始准备吧，不要把所有的事情都拖延到明天。你已选择了更好的方向，为人生的新里程碑展开挑战，所以现在是你下定决心、大步迈进的时候了。

How to use this book

Speaking Overview 口试介绍

This is designed to provide a general understanding of what happens in the official test. The more familiar you are with the test proceedings, the less nervous and more confident you will feel in the real test.

此部分提供口语测试的方式及流程，你越熟悉测试方式，应试时就会越有信心。

FAQs 常见问题集

Although you've probably done a bit of research on IELTS already, I'm sure you still have a number of questions unanswered. The FAQs has been compiled by IELTS examiners, IELTS teachers, IELTS consultants and IELTS students with the aim of putting your nerves at ease.

常见问题集由口试官、IELTS 资深教师、顾问以及学生协力完成，解答考生对 IELTS 的各种疑惑。

Marking Criteria 口试的 4 个评分标准

This will highlight the examiners' expectations of candidates, let you know what will be penalised and what won't and what you should and shouldn't do.

口试的 4 个评分标准可提醒考生注意口试时不能犯哪些错误，有哪些错误会被扣分，哪些不会。

Sample Interviews 口试现场模拟

These have been provided with "comments" to give you a deeper insight into how the examiner will assess your performance. The IELTS 9 samples include the scripts.

提供各个分数级别的考生口试模拟示范及评分表，帮助考生进一步了解评分规则。9 分的示范附有完整对话内容。

Do It Yourself Study Guide 口语能力——自学要诀

After hearing other students' weaknesses and thinking about your own, you can use the study tips to help you plan your study schedule. Tips are provided for each criterion of the speaking test.

此部分提供针对口试 4 个评分标准的个别准备方式，供考生自我练习。

Speaking Test: Part 1 口试第一部分

This will introduce the most common question types encountered in Part 1 and give you tips on how to state and develop your opinion using the QPS strategy.

本部分会教考生如何应用 QPS 应考策略回答 Part 1 的常见问题。

Speaking Test: Part 2 口试第二部分

This will advise you on the best way to make notes and the most common types of topic cards. Sample answers are provided on how your notes turn into a short presentation.

此部分提供 Part 2 常见考题，并指导考生做笔记，进而将笔记整理成一篇完整的表达。

Speaking Test: Part 3 口试第三部分

This will introduce the most common question types encountered in Part 3 and give you tips on how to state and develop your opinion again using the QPS strategy.

此部分收录 Part 3 常见问题，并指导考生利用 QPS 应考策略发展意见。

Test Bank with Sample Answers 题库与 9 分口语范例

There are 8 mock speaking tests included for extra practice. Sample answers are also provided for your reference so that you can have a better idea on how a native speaker would answer the interview questions.

此部分提供 8 篇全真口语模拟试题与范例。口试中回答的部分为专业外籍教师的 9 分示范，供考生参考。

Topic-Based Question Bank 主题分类问题集

There are general topics, as well as subtopics, for Parts 1, 2 and 3 which are given primarily to build your vocabulary and confidence on the most common themes encountered in the official test. In the real test questions will be arranged randomly and not by topic. Therefore, some "Official Samples", located after the sample interviews, and after this Question Bank, have also been compiled to give you an idea of the variety of questions that will be asked.

此部分提供正式考试中常考主题问题集。在 IELTS 正式测试中，问题不局限于一种主题，故此部分可帮助考生熟悉各种主题。

Cut-Up Study Notes 随身学习卡

These have been compiled so that you can review everything conveniently anytime, anywhere.

随身学习卡提供考生随时随地复习各种问题及答题的方式。

Topic-Based Glossary 主题分类实用词汇

The following vocabulary, if used correctly, would typify some of the vocabulary an IELTS 7 and above candidate would produce. It has been arranged according to topic and includes a number of idioms.

考生若能正确应用此部分的词汇及惯用语，就说明已具备 IELTS 7 分及以上的英语能力。

Introduction of Speakers' Accents 录音员口音介绍

In the IELTS test you will hear a range of accents, as the exam tests international English—not just British. Oral examiners also have varying backgrounds so it is important that you expose yourself to a number of different accents in order to perform well in the IELTS.

IELTS 的口试官来自各个国家，考生有可能会遇到有各种口音的口试官。本书特别挑选来自各个不同国家的专业录音员，以帮助考生熟悉口试时可能会遇到的各种口音。

Recordist	Accent	Track
Jez (Waterloo, England)	**standard British**	MP3 02–08
Petula (south west England)	**standard British**	MP3 13
Mark (Bristol, England)	**standard British**	MP3 14, 18
Jessica (America)	**American**	MP3 15, 20
Patrick (Brisbane, Australia)	**Australian**	MP3 16, 21
David (South Africa)	**South African**	MP3 17, 19
John (Newcastle, England)	**northern (Geordie) British**	MP3 22–23
Natasha (Auckland, New Zealand)	**New Zealand**	MP3 24–25
Mark (Brighton, England)	**standard British**	MP3 26–27
Catherine (Manchester, England)	**standard British**	MP3 28–29
Matthew (north east England)	**slightly northern British**	MP3 30–31
Olivia (Pretoria, South Africa)	**South African**	MP3 32–33

英式音标・KK 音标对照表

元音	
英式音标	KK 音标
[ɪ]	[ɪ]
[e]	[ɛ]
[æ]	[æ]
[ɒ]	[ɑ], [ɔ]
[ʌ]	[ʌ]
[ʊ]	[ʊ]
[ə]	[ə], [ɚ]
[i]	[ɪ]
[u]	[u]
[iː]	[i]
[ɑː]	[ɑ], [ɑr]
[ɔː]	[ɔ], [ɔr]
[uː]	[u]
[ɜː]	[ɝ]
[eɪ]	[e]
[aɪ]	[aɪ]
[ɔɪ]	[ɔɪ]
[əʊ]	[o]
[oʊ]	[o]
[aʊ]	[au]
[ɪə]	[ɪr]
[eə]	[ɛr]
[ʊə]	[ʊr]
[iə]	[jɚ]

辅音	
英式音标	KK 音标
[p]	[p]
[b]	[b]
[t]	[t]
[d]	[d]
[k]	[k]
[f]	[f]
[v]	[v]
[θ]	[θ]
[ð]	[ð]
[s]	[s]
[z]	[z]
[ʃ]	[ʃ]
[ʒ]	[ʒ]
[h]	[h]
[k]	[k]
[tʃ]	[tʃ]
[dʒ]	[dʒ]
[m]	[m]
[n]	[n]
[ŋ]	[ŋ]
[w]	[w]
[l]	[l]
[r]	[r]
[j]	[j]

About IELTS

IELTS（International English Language Testing System）"国际英语语言测试系统"是全球认可的英语语言能力评估系统，也是进入大多数英语系国家高等学府就读必备的英语能力证明，尤为英国、澳大利亚、新西兰、加拿大等国的教育系统所接受，而目前美国大多数大学也承认IELTS成绩。IELTS测试分为"学术类"（Academic）与"培训类"（General Training），测验项目涵盖听、读、说、写，内容丰富、全面而多元，因此也可作一般性英语能力检测之用。除了计划前往英语系国家就读大学、研究生院、专科技术学院、预科课程者适合参加IELTS测试外，凡申请澳大利亚、新西兰、加拿大、美国移民者，或是担任英国及澳大利亚各政府部门实习生、参加国防部及公共医疗会议等的专业人士，都可以参加IELTS测试。IELTS测试由英国文化协会（The British Council）、剑桥大学考试委员会 （Cambridge ESOL）及澳大利亚教育国际开发署（IDP Education Australia）共同举办，由Cambridge ESOL统筹管理。

IELTS 测试方式

IELTS测试分为学术类（Academic）和培训类（General Training），测试内容分为听、读、说、写四部分，其中Listening和Speaking部分不分类，Reading和Writing两项则分类。

■ 学术类（Academic）

主要用来评估考生在攻读本科或研究生等课程时，是否适合以英语作为学习的媒介。

■ 培训类（General Training）

适合前往英语系国家就读中学、工作或参与非学术单位培训计划的考生，许多国家也用以评估申请移民人士的英语程度。

IELTS 测试流程图

IELTS测试分为听力、阅读、写作、口语四部分，测试时间为2小时54分钟。

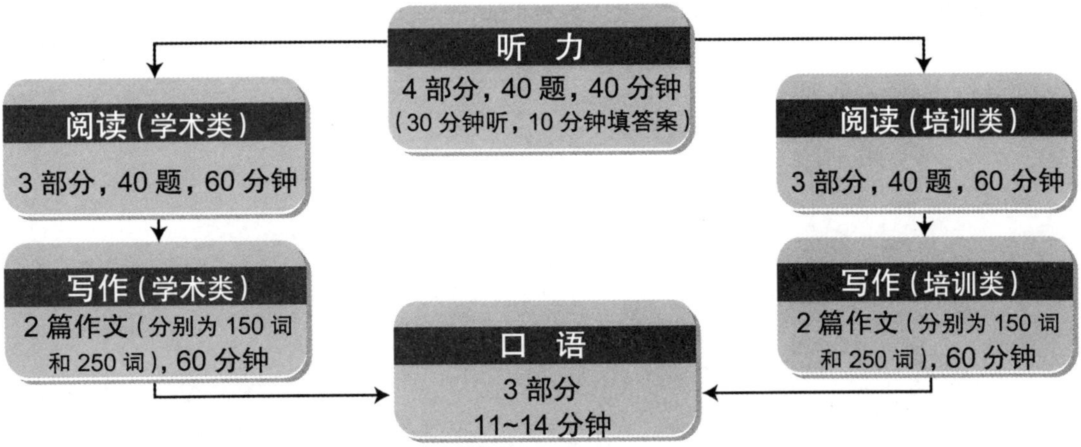

IELTS 测试内容

■ IELTS Listening Module·听力

内容	· 测试时间 40 分钟，其中 10 分钟填答案 · 分为 4 部分，共有 40 题 · 听力只放一遍，不会重复
题型结构	· 第一、二段：以一般生活及社会状态为主 · 第三、四段：涵盖教育、学术、世界性的主题 · 题型：选择题、填空题、简答题、图表题
作答重点	· 要边听边作答 · 需了解独白或对话的主题 · 注意数字、时间、日期等较明显的字眼 · 听出重要的词句，记下与主题相关或有因果关系的信息

■ IELTS Reading Module·阅读

内容	· 测试时间 1 小时，含填写答案时间 · 包含 3 篇文章，每篇约有 700～900 词 · 测试题目共 40 题
题型结构	· 主题多样化，除了日常生活，还包括学术上的探讨与了解 · 题型：简答题、选择题、匹配题、填空题、图表题、表格题、段落大意题、摘要题、是 / 非 / 未提及题（True/False/Not Given或Yes/No/Not Given）
作答重点	· 了解各段落主题与大意 · 圈出重要信息 · 圈出数字、日期、时间、项目等较明显的词句 · 不需要了解每一个单词的意思，不要浪费时间推敲不明白的地方

■ IELTS Writing Module·写作

内容	· 测试时间 1 小时，需写 2 篇作文 · Task 1：最少 150 词，建议花 20 分钟 · Task 2：最少 250 词，建议花 40 分钟
题型结构	· Task 1：考题基本形式为图片、表格、曲线图、饼状图等，考生依照所给的信息，分析、组织并讨论主题 · Task 2：依照所给的主题，表达自己的意见、支持或反驳、解决问题及讨论问题
作答重点	Task 1： · 避免使用自己没把握的单词和语法结构 · 从题目要求中，清楚分析题目，圈出重要的词或短语 Task 2： · 仔细阅读题目，避免文不对题 · 强调自己的想法和意见 · 支持或反对考题的论点，只能二选一，定位要清楚

■ IELTS Speaking Module·口试

内容	· 测试时间约11～14分钟，分成3个部分 Part 1：4～5分钟，自我介绍及面谈 Part 2：3～4分钟，1分钟准备，对特定话题发表看法 Part 3：4～5分钟，第二部分的延伸讨论，题目较第二部分抽象
题型结构	· Part 1：口试官介绍自己并确认考生身份，询问考生与个人有关的事物、家人、兴趣、工作背景等 · Part 2：口试官出示话题卡，考生依据话题卡可有1分钟的准备时间，考场备有纸笔供考生使用 · Part 3：连结第二部分的延伸讨论，或更深更广的互动讨论
作答重点	· 有效表达意见，与口试官沟通 · 正确使用词汇和语法 · 能够参与一般对话或勇于发问、发言 · 轻松应对，表达流畅，答为所问

IELTS 测试的一天

■ 笔试部分

时　间	考场建议
在早上8:00前 到达考场	· 请在考试当天上午8:00前到达考试中心。8:30以后停止进场。8:30以后到达考场的考生将被取消参加笔试的资格，并不得转考、退考或退费。笔试迟到的考生有权利选择参加口语考试。 · 在考场张贴的名单上找到自己的名字，记住自己的考场。 · 听从考试中心工作人员的指挥到候考室候考。 · 仔细听考试中心的工作人员介绍考前的注意事项。
入场 上午8:00 到 8:30	· 遵照考试中心工作人员的安排在教室外按照考号顺序排队等候。请在排队前先上洗手间。 · 在进入教室前准备好您的身份证和一张护照照片尺寸的彩照待检。彩照必须是6个月内的近照，且背面要写上您的名字和考号。请将您的私人物品存放在指定的区域。 · 根据桌上的标签找到您的位置。 · 请就座。您可以利用这段时间测试一下您的耳机。
准备考试 上午8:30 到 9:00	· 在所有考生就坐后，监考人员会开始宣读考试事项。 · 您的身份证会被暂时集中收起，并在笔试结束前发还给您。 · 监考人员会给您分发听力/阅读答题纸。请根据指示填好答题纸(听力部分和阅读部分的答题区分别在答题纸的正反两面)。 · 根据指示测试您的耳机。 · 监考人员将分发听力试卷并要求您在封面填写姓名和考号。 · 听力考试录音中会提示您何时打开试卷。在此之前，您不可以打开试卷。 · 在考试正式开始以前，监考人员还会要求您再次检查耳机。
考试进行中 上午9:00到12:00	· 考试于早上9:00正式开始。 · 请注意听从监考人员的指示。 · 如果您有疑问，请举手向监考人员示意寻求帮助。 · 如果您认为您得到的试卷有误，或是试卷缺页、模糊，请马上告诉监考人员。 · 在考试进行期间，您不能和其他考生互借文具。 · 当您听到停止作答的指示时，请马上停止答卷，并放下铅笔。否则您将被视为违反考试规则，可能被取消考试成绩。

■ 口试部分

- 请在您预定的口试时间前 30 分钟到达考试中心并签到。未能在考试前 15 分钟到达并签到的考生，将有可能被取消参加口试的资格，并不得转考、退考或退费。
- 请带上您的身份证参加口试。
- 听从工作人员的指挥，在候考室待考。工作人员会带领您到口试考场。请在口试考场外等候考官请您进入。
- 口试考试时间为 11 到 14 分钟。
- 在完成口试后，请立即离开考场。不要与任何人谈及您的考试情况，否则可能会被视做违反考场纪律。

■ 考试建议

- 您可以在考试日前4天从NEEA IELTS 报名网站（http://ielts.etest.net.cn）上查看您的考号和口试时间，并打印准考证。
- 请您在参加考试前仔细阅读《中国地区IELTS考生须知》。
- 请您带上身份证明，一张护照尺寸的6个月内的彩照（照片后面附上您的姓名和考号），以及您的准考证到考场。
- 您在笔试和口试入场前均须出示与报名时一致的有效身份证件，出示与报名信息不符证件的考生将有可能不能参加考试，并不得转考、退考或退费。
- 强烈建议您不要携带手机或其他电子通讯类产品进入考场。所有电子、通讯设备禁止带入考场，即使已呈关闭状态。这一规定同时适用于笔试和口试。任何携带电子、通讯设备进入考场的考生，一律取消考试资格。
- 除了需要检验身份证和照片之外，考生禁止携带任何私人物品进入考场。此规定同时适用于笔试和口试。请不要携带任何贵重物品到考场，考生的个人物品将被存放在考场以外的指定地点。英国文化协会中国办公室（英国驻华使/领馆文化教育处）和考试中心恕不对考生个人物品的损失或遗失负责。

IELTS 测试成绩计算方式

IELTS 测试分为 Listening、Reading、Writing 和 Speaking 四项，此四项皆独立计分，最后再以四个分数合计，除以四而得一平均分数，所以在成绩单上会列出每项的分数和平均分数。IELTS 的满分为 9 分，若成绩达 Band 9，表示该考生能自如地运用英语，具备在英语语言国家学习的能力。反之，若成绩是 Band 1，则表示该考生不具有在英语语言国家学习的英语能力。每所学术机构要求的最低入学成绩不尽相同，一般来说，大部分学校会要求学生至少具备 IELTS 6.0~6.5 或同等程度的入学标准。

■ 计算方式

四大项都有 0.5 分(如 5.5，6.5)。

总分：将四项得分平均后，除 0.5 分外，每 0.25 进一个单位(0.5)

	例一	例二	例三
听力 Listening Band	7.0	6.0	6.0
阅读 Reading Band	6.0	6.0	5.5
写作 Writing Band	6.5	7.0	5.5
口试 Speaking Band	7.5	7.0	5.5
平均	(7.0+6.0+6.5+7.5)/4 =6.75(可进位)	(6.0+6.0+7.0+7.0)/4 =6.5	(6.0+5.5+5.5+5.5)/4 =5.625(不可进位)
总分	7	6.5	5.5

■ 考试成绩与成绩单发放

雅思考试成绩单是考生英语能力的权威证明，显示考生听力、阅读、写作和口语4个分项的成绩以及总成绩。雅思考试成绩自考试之日起2年内有效。

考生须正常完成笔试、口试所有科目及如期参加现场照相方可以收到成绩单。考生可以在笔试后第10个工作日登录教育部考试中心雅思报名网站“我的状态”页面查看考试成绩。考生成绩单将同时通过EMS(仅限于中国大陆地区服务)寄往考生报名时提供的成绩单寄送地址，每位考生只能收到1份成绩单原件。

■ 额外成绩单申请与寄送

成绩公布后，考生可以登录雅思官网考后服务平台在线申请寄送额外成绩单并支付相关费用。额外成绩单在线寄送申请一旦提交成功无法更改或取消。从2012年1月7日起参加考试的考生，雅思成绩2年有效期内申请的前5份额外成绩单寄送将免除人民币60元/份的普通服务手续费用。从第6份额外成绩单起，普通服务手续费为人民币60元/份。

■ 成绩复议

若欲复议成绩，考生需在收到成绩单后，登录“雅思官网考后服务平台”在线申请成绩复议服务，并支付相关费用1000元。同时，还需将成绩单原件寄送到雅思考试全国考后服务热线，收件人是英国大使馆文化教育处考试部。复议服务申请时限为考试日期后6周内。

若复议结果高于原成绩，则复议费用全数退还；若成绩相同或低于原分数，则复议费用不予退还。

IELTS

SUPERIOR SPEAKING

口试介绍与模拟示范

IELTS Speaking Test Introduction and Sample Interviews

Introduction to the Speaking Section of IELTS

IELTS 口试介绍

Overview
口试流程

There are 3 parts to the IELTS speaking section, which increases in difficulty and runs for a total of 11-14 minutes.

IELTS 口语测试分为 3 个部分，难度递增，全程 11～14 分钟。

Part 1
(4-5 minutes)

- **Introductions** *MP3 02*

  This will include greetings and checking of candidate's ID.

  问候并确认考生身份。

- **Hometowns or jobs/studies** *MP3 03*

  Candidates are asked around 3 questions on one of the aforementioned topics.

  考生会被问及约 3 个有关考生的家乡、工作或学业等的问题。

- **General topics** *MP3 04*

  Candidates are asked between 3-6 questions from another 1 or 2 general topics.

  考生接着会再被问到几个一般性问题。

Part 2
(3-4 minutes)

- **Explanation** *MP3 05*

  The examiner will introduce Part 2 and hand candidates a topic card, paper and pen.

  口试官会介绍口试 Part 2 的测试方式，并给考生 1 张话题卡及纸笔。

- **Preparation time** *MP3 05*

  Candidates are given 1 minute to make notes on the given topic.

  考生有 1 分钟的准备时间，为话题做笔记。

- **Individual long turns** *MP3 06*

  Candidates are required to give a speech for 1-2 minutes.

  考生针对主题发表 1～2 分钟的意见。

Part 3
(4-5 minutes)

■ **Follow up question** *MP3 07*

If time allows, the examiner will ask candidates a question to bring Part 2 to an end.

若时间允许，口试官会再问考生 1 个问题，作为 Part 2 的结束。

■ **Discussion** *MP3 08*

Candidates will be asked a few more questions which are related to the Part 2 topic. This is often the section which makes or breaks candidates.

考生会被问到几个与 Part 2 主题相关的问题，这个部分通常较为困难。

Possible IELTS Band 9
9 分(参考分数)

Part 1 *MP3 02–08*

Hello, my name is (examiner's name).
What's your full name please?
Can I check your ID and passport please?
In the first part, I'd like to ask you some general questions about yourself.

Let's talk about your work or school.
- Are you a student or do you work?
- Do you like your school?
- Is there anything you would like to change about your school?
- How do you travel to school?

Let's move on to email.
- How often do you use email?
- Do you think writing an email is better than writing a letter?

Now I'd like to ask you about travel.
- What countries have you travelled to before?
- Where wouldn't you like to travel to? Why not?

Part 2

In Part 2, I will give you a topic and I'd like you to talk about it for 1-2 minutes. Before you talk, you will have one minute to think about what you are going to say. You may make some notes if you wish. Do you understand?

Topic Card

Describe a problem in your city.
You should say:
- what it is
- how it was caused
- why it is a problem

and offer some solutions to the problem.

- Are you optimistic that the situation will improve?

Part 3

You've been talking about a problem in your city and I'd like to ask you one or two more questions related to this. Let's consider first of all:

The development of cities
- Examine the causes of urbanisation.
- Predict how cities will develop in the future.

Global issues
- Describe how noticeable the gap between the rich and the poor is in your country.
- Discuss how worried you are about rising world temperatures.

Thank you. That is the end of the speaking test.

SCRIPT 对话内容

Part 1

Hello, my name is Christopher. What's your full name please?

My name is Jeremy David Hellard.

OK. And can I check your ID and passport① please?

Yes, certainly.

Thank you. That's fine. In the first part, I'd like to ask you some general questions about yourself. Let's talk about your work or school. Are you a student or do you work?

I'm a student.

And do you like your school?

Yeah, I like, I like my school. I like studying there but the actual building, the actual surroundings are nothing special. We tend to call it "Strand Poly" rather than King's College.

And is there anything you would like to change about your school?

There are certainly a lot of things that could be changed about King's College. To start with as I said it's, it's not the most beautiful place yet it is next to a wonderful London building called Northumberland House and ours looks drab and black by comparison. And apart from that we have a very famous War Studies department that actually trains a lot of rather dubious dictators and other characters from countries that I would rather not have my university train people from. So there are a couple of issues I think we could change.

How do you travel to school?

I walk across the bridge because I live very close to King's College in

① 注：在中国内地考试，通常需要带身份证或护照、准考证和一张护照尺寸的6月内的彩照。

Waterloo so I walk across Waterloo Bridge and see the trail of drips of blood and, and rather dubious fluids which you see lying on the roads there. So yeah I walk just a short distance.

Now let's move on to email. How often do you use email?

Email. I tend to use email about once or twice a week just to keep in touch with people who I'm not in the same city as or the same country as at the moment.

Do you think writing an email is better than writing a letter?

I don't think it's better than writing a letter. I much prefer writing and receiving letters but the emails are so much more useful for immediate communication. So if I really need to get in touch with people or more than one person at a time then I might well prefer to use email because it's slightly more efficient in the modern setting.

Now I'd like to ask you about travel. What countries have you travelled to before?

I've travelled extensively in Europe and Asia but never outside of these 2 continents so I've been to most Western European countries: Germany, France, Spain, Switzerland, Holland, Belgium, Luxembourg, Italy, Czechoslovakia and in Asia I've spent most of the time in India, Nepal, Thailand, Laos.

And where wouldn't you like to travel to?

I wouldn't like to go to Los Angeles or the suburban sprawl around that area. I tend to, I would love to go to the United States for a lot of reasons but I think that absolute height of modern suburbanisation that is Los Angeles County is something that I would rather never see.

Part 2

OK, let's move on to Part 2. In Part 2, I will give you a topic and I'd like you to talk about it for 1-2 minutes. Before you talk, you will have one minute to think about what you are going to say. You may make some notes if you wish. Do you understand?

I understand yes.

So here's your topic. I'd like you to describe a problem in your city.

Well, I think that the main problem that I see with London is congestion of traffic. Because despite all of the new congestion laws which have been installed in recent times, I find that the very nature of London is that it is an old city, about one or two thousand years old in its present size and sprawl, obviously it's grown a little. But it is designed around the idea of having horses and carts, ponies and traps trundling through the cobbled streets saying good morning to each other in a nice English style. But now we have thousands and thousands of jeeps, sports utility vehicles and other oversized vehicles which were designed for American ranches driving through our cities. So London in particular, as you get to the centre, it becomes a complete gridlock where you breathe diesel fuel all the time and when you get home you will blow black dust out of your nose. So I think although there are a lot of other problems in the metropolitan situation, I tend to find that in London it's definitely the overflow of vehicles and people who decide rather than using the public transport that they want to take their own car and listen to their own music on their own stereo system. So basically I think this is the nature of the problems with my city.

OK, and are you optimistic that the situation will improve?

No, not really. They're trying, as I say they've installed congestion charges and laws to prevent it from happening but people will just shoulder that cost, people will simply say "I have to pay five pounds more each time I go to town". So they will pay five pounds more but the problem remains until they pedestrianise the centre of the city.

Part 3

OK, thank you. Now let's move on to Part 3. You've been talking about a problem in your city and I'd like to ask you one or two more questions related to this. So let's consider first of all the development of cities. Could you examine the causes of urbanisation?

Well the causes of urbanisation are basically the industrial revolution which started I suppose in English cities. But when London's East End started to industrialise, then obviously they need hundreds of thousands of workers to run the factories and the massive infrastructure of the port city which is London which for certainly a century or so was one of the busiest ports in the entire world. So the amount of people who had to come from the British countryside or from other countries altogether, often places which had been previously colonised by Britain. These people were all drawn towards the centre of industry and therefore we get two things happening. One is a massive overcrowding therefore a likeliness for easily transmitted diseases or just a lack of cleanliness that you might find in a food market with too many rats, but the other side of the problem is, is so many communities who are entirely different in their cultural outlook living next door to each other and sometimes this works very well but other times we can see eruptions of sporadic violence or malcontent amongst different social groups.

And could you speculate on how cities will develop in the future?

I think cities will probably develop upwards in the same way as we have seen in American cities that buildings will become taller with better security guards and more windows so that people can live in the city with the convenience of the local 7-11 without having to encounter the chock-a-block street side life that you will find in any modern metropolis.

And let's talk about some global issues. Could you describe how noticeable the gap between the rich and the poor is in your country?

Yes, it's certainly very noticeable and I would quote a prominent conservative politician who said "The homeless! Oh they're the people we step over when we come out of the opera". So in, in London particularly and also

Manchester and Birmingham you can really see a lot of people who are sleeping in the street on newspapers whilst right next to them are extremely wealthy London bankers or Arab oil men, people with chauffeurs, people with people to carry the back of their coat over the homeless people so as not to tarnish it. So I think it's very obvious the difference between rich and the poor particularly if you go closer to the centre of urbanised areas.

And how worried are you about rising world temperatures?

Well I think it's certainly worrying. The trend of global warming, so called, also in other parts of the world we'll see global cooling so it's not simply the idea of I'm worried about temperatures rising. If you look in the centre of Canada at the moment there's a massive cold snap which is harder than is usually expected at this time of year. So I think that global warming is more complex than perhaps just rising world temperatures. But certainly I'm worried that we have done something to the balance of our world's equilibrium, so to say, that we might not be able to repair.

Thank you. That is the end of the speaking test.

Frequently Asked Questions (FAQs)

常见问题集

Scoring
评分标准

1. How is my performance assessed?

口试官的评分标准是什么?

Examiners will evaluate your performance according to 4 criteria namely fluency and coherence (FC), lexical resource (LR), grammatical range and accuracy (GRA) and pronunciation (P).

口试官会依照 4 个部分评分：流畅性及连贯性（FC）、词汇量（LR）、语法运用范围与其正确性(GRA)以及发音(P)。

2. What is the most important criterion in the speaking test? Is it grammar?

口语测试中最重要的是语法吗?

No. The 4 criteria are weighted equally at 25% each. The examiners will give a result for each criterion and then work out the average of the 4 scores which equates to an overall speaking score. If you get 6 for FC, 5 for LR, 5 for GRA and 6 for P, then you will receive 5.5 overall for speaking.

不是。4 个评分标准同等重要，各占 25%。口试官会针对这 4 个部分分别评分，然后计算出 1 个平均分数；若你在 FC 拿到 6 分、LR 和 GRA 都拿到 5 分、P 拿到 6 分，那你会拿到总分 5.5分。

3. Will I lose points if the examiner disagrees with my opinion?

如果口试官不认同我的想法，我会被扣分吗?

No. You are judged on your English, not your opinions. There is no right or wrong opinion.

不会。口试的评分标准是你的英文能力，而非想法，更无论对错了。

4. I'm not very opinionated ... Can I still get a good score?

我不是个有主见的人，这样也可以拿到高分吗?

Yes. As long as you keep talking and use a wide range of English, you can get a high score as this is not an IQ test. Boring or obvious opinions are fine if you can produce a wide and accurate range of language when expressing them.

当然可以。只要你持续不断地用正确的英文来表达自己的想法，即可得到高分，即使是乏味的想法也没关系，因为这并不是智力测验。

5. I have a North American accent, is that OK?

我有美国口音，这样可以吗?

Yes. American English is not penalised in any part of the test whether it be pronunciation or spelling.

可以。美国口音或拼写并不会影响评分。

6. Can I ask my examiner what score he/she will give me?

我可以问口试官会给我几分吗?

No. You will receive your IELTS result within 2 weeks, or you can check the result online after 13 days.

不行。IELTS 的成绩会在测试后 2 个星期之内收到；也可以在测试后 13 天上网查询。

7. What happens if I disagree with the result I was given?

如果我对口试成绩有疑问怎么办?

You may ask the IELTS test centre to arrange another IELTS examiner to reevaluate your speaking. This is possible as all interviews are recorded. You may incur an extra expense depending on whether your score changes or not.

口试的部分都有录音，故可要求考试中心重新评估口试的成绩。若口试成绩经过复议后并没有更改，你须支付额外的复议费；反之，则不必支付。

8. Is it better to do the speaking test in my home country or in England/Australia, etc.?

在自己的国家参加口试会比在其他国家好吗?

In your home country is often thought to be the best place to do the speaking test. However, do keep in mind that all examiners receive exactly the same training around the world which is moderated by a central body. The only justification for why it may be better to do the test in your home country is that you may score higher in pronunciation as it is seen as more subjective; examiners in your home country will be used to the Chinese accent whereas those in England may not.

在自己的国家考试通常被认为是最好的。然而请记住,全世界所有的 IELTS 口试官接受的都是相同的训练。在自己国家考试较好的唯一理由,就是在发音部分会较占优势,例如在中国的口试官势必比较习惯考生有中国的口音。

The Questions & Answers
关于问与答

1. Is there anything I can do if I don't understand a question?

假如我听不懂口试官的问题，该怎么办?

Yes. If you don't understand you may ask the examiner to repeat the question at any time during the interview. However, if after repeating you still don't understand, only in Part 3 may you ask the examiner to explain or rephrase a question. In Part 1 the examiner will simply move on to the next question.

假若你不明白问题，可以请口试官再复述一次。但如果口试官重复后，你还是不理解，只有在 Part 3 时你才可以请口试官换个说法让你明白问题；在口试的 Part 1，口试官会略过该问题而直接进行下一个提问。

2. What happens if I misunderstand the question?

如果我误会了问题的意思，结果会如何?

You may lose some points under fluency and coherence as the examiner may have difficulty following your answer. In Part 3 the examiner may rephrase or explain the question again to give you a second opportunity. This will not happen in Part 1 though, the examiner will move on to the next question.

你可能会在流畅性及连贯性这部分被扣分。在 Part 3，口试官有可能会再重述或解释该题，给你第二次机会回答；但是在 Part 1 时，口试官会直接问你下一个问题。

3. What should I do if I can't think of the right vocabulary?

假如我想不出合适的词汇表达时该怎么办?

Keep talking by paraphrasing (explaining the meaning of the word). It's better to say something than nothing. If you simply pause and hope that somehow the word miraculously pops into your head, the examiner will be unable to assess you. In other words, long silences are penalised in each criterion as you are producing no vocabulary, grammar or pronunciation features and showing no fluency.

利用你会的词句代替或解释你想不出来的词汇，这比什么都不说要好，口试官是不会让你停顿下来思考你要的词汇的；换句话说，沉默或间断的应答在 4 个评分标准下都无法得分。

4. Can I make up an answer or lie in the test?

在考试当中我可以编造答案或说谎吗？

Preferably not. Although there is no way of knowing if you are telling the truth or not, it's OK to be honest and more importantly you will sound much more natural and fluent if you are. Just remember to use good English. If the examiner asks you if you like your hometown, you don't need to pretend that you do if you don't. It's quite fine to say you hate it as long as you do so using appropriate English. Similarly if the examiner asks you if you have ever had a pet, but you never have, then say so and give a reason why you haven't.

最好不要。因为真实的回答听起来会比较自然且流畅，重点在于你是否能用好的英文来表达；举例来说，当口试官问你是否喜欢你的家乡，或你是否养过宠物时，你可以回答不喜欢或是你没养过宠物，只要说明原因即可。

5. Can I ask the examiner questions?

我可以问口试官问题吗？

Yes and No. You may ask the examiner to repeat or rephrase a question but do not ask him/her about their opinions. The test examines your English, not the examiner's. You only have 11-14 minutes to show the examiner the full range of English you have learnt over the past 5 years or so, so don't waste your precious time listening to the examiner.

视情况而定。如果听不清楚题目，你可以请口试官复述一次，但不能问口试官的想法。重点是“你才是考试的主角”。你只有 11～14 分钟的时间来表现你的英文能力，让口试官发表意见而浪费了你的宝贵时间并不是明智之举。

6. Is it OK to memorise my answers?

可以背答案吗？

No. There is no way of knowing exactly what questions will be asked and therefore you may give inappropriate answers if you simply regurgitate memorised answers. Nevertheless, some common phrases that could be used in a variety of situations are definitely OK to memorise.

不可以。你绝不可能准确地预测到口试的题目，请你记住："计划永远赶不上变化！"但你还是可以熟记一些惯用语，并且在考试当中灵活运用。

7. Should I be relaxed and easygoing or serious and formal?

考试时，我应该表现得轻松自在还是正襟危坐？

Try to be relaxed. You don't need to sound academic in the speaking interview. Just imagine that you are discussing the interview questions with your friend so that you sound more natural and fluent. Examiners are your friends!

试着让自己放轻松。如果太紧张，可能会导致无法充分发挥原有的英文能力。把口试官想象成你的朋友，轻松自然地回答即可。

8. Is it OK to give short answers to avoid making too many mistakes?

我可以简答以避免犯太多的错误吗？

No. Try to give full, extended, complete answers and sentences. You need to demonstrate as much English as possible in the time given.

建议不要。应该在有限的时间里尽量完整并充分地回答问题，以展现你的英文能力。

9. How much should I say?

我应该讲多久?

In Part 1 you have 4-5 minutes to answer at least 3 and up to 10 questions which works out to between 20 to 90 seconds per question but do not rely on slow speech to fill up this time. In Part 2 you must speak for 1-2 minutes and it is advisable that you speak closer to 2 minutes than 1. The examiner is required to stop you if you speak for longer than 2 minutes for which you will not be penalised. In Part 3 you have 4-5 minutes to answer between 2-6 questions which works out to between 40 to 150 seconds per answer. Try to find a happy medium between these time frames so that you can answer a range of questions as this will produce a wider range of language.

在 Part 1，花 4～5 分钟的时间回答 3～10 个题目，每个题目大概花 20～90 秒完成，不要试图通过放慢说话速度来拉长时间；在 Part 2，你需要花 1～2 分钟的时间发表意见，如果你的回答超过时限，口试官会喊停，但你不会因此被扣分；在 Part 3，口试官会问 2～6 个题目，你有 4～5 分钟的时间，每个题目需要 40～150 秒的时间回答。记住：要视当下的状况而定，好好掌握能充分展现你英文能力的时间。

10. Do I need to speak really quickly?

我需要讲得很快吗?

No. Just speak at a steady, constant speed which can balance your fluency and accuracy.

不需要。用一般的速度、有条不紊地回答即可，记住以表达清楚为主。

11. Will I be recorded?

口试过程会录音吗?

Yes. For quality control and reassessment purposes all interviews are recorded.

会。为了评分的准确与公正性，以及日后复议等，口试会全程录音。

Examiners
关于口试官

1. Do all examiners have a British accent?

所有的口试官都是英式口音吗?

No. Examiners come from a variety of backgrounds and therefore accents may vary. You may even have a Chinese examiner if they themselves have scored an IELTS 9 on the test.

不是。口试官来自不同的国家,有各自不同的口音。你也可能遇到口试成绩满分的中国考官。

2. How many examiners will listen to me?

应考时,会有几位口试官?

One during the interview but another examiner may listen to your recording for reassessing or monitoring.

应考时,只会面对 1 位口试官。

3. Can I choose which examiner I want?

我可以选择口试官吗?

No. Examiners will be arranged for candidates in a random order. If you know the examiner in any way, he/she may not assess you under any circumstances.

不可以。口试官是主办单位随机分派的,如果你认识口试官,他 / 她是不能为你进行口试的。

4. Are some examiners stricter than others?

有些口试官特别严格吗?

No. All examiners have received the same training so all results are standardised. While some may look stricter, their scoring won't be.

不会。所有的口试官都接受一样的训练,所以他们的评分标准是一致的;虽然有的口试官看起来较严肃,但评分标准并不会因此较严格。

The IELTS Speaking Test
关于 IELTS 口试

1. Is the interview the same for both the General Training Module and Academic Module?

培训类的口试与学术类的口试是相同的吗?

Yes. There is no difference between the 2 modules in the speaking section. It is exactly the same.

是的,完全相同。

2. Is it best to do the speaking test on the same day or on separate days?

口试在笔试当日考较好,还是另外选一天?

It's up to you. Do you prefer to get the test over and done with on the same day? It may prolong your stress and nerves. Is it convenient for you to take the test over a number of days? You must take into account the location of the test centre and/or if you have the time to go to the centre on two seperate days. An extra day of preparation will have very minimal effect on your overall level.

由你决定。你比较喜欢在同一天完成所有的考试吗?那样也许会让你的压力和紧张再延续一段时间。过几天后再考口试,对你来说会更方便些吗?那你必须考虑是否有时间再前往考试中心。其实,多几天的时间准备口试,对你的总体水平影响不大。

3. Is the TOEFL speaking the same as the IELTS speaking?

TOEFL 的口试和 IELTS 的口试一样吗?

No. The speaking section of TOEFL is an integrated skills test in which they combine your listening, reading and speaking skills. There is no live interview with an examiner in the TOEFL.

不一样。TOEFL 口试考查考生听、读、说的综合技能,而且是以机考形式来进行,并没有口试官。

4. Which section of IELTS speaking is the most difficult?

口试的哪个部分最难?

Part 3 is the most difficult section of the speaking as examiners will ask you questions on unfamiliar, more academic topics.

在 Part 3，口试官会问一些对你而言较陌生或较学术的问题。

5. What do I need to bring into the interview room with me?

口试时，需要带些什么东西吗?

Your ID card, test centre ID and a passport-sized photograph taken within the previous 6 months for the examiner to check and a positive attitude.

身份证、准考证和一张 6 个月内的护照尺寸的彩照以及最有把握的态度。

6. What should I wear?

考试当天我应该穿什么?

It's neither a fashion show nor a board meeting with the directors. Just wear something you feel comfortable in (smart casual) as you only want to be concerned with your English not your clothes.

你只需要穿上你觉得最舒服的衣服(看起来较正式的休闲服)。你要花心思的是你的英文，而非穿着。

Preparation
关于考前准备

1. Is it possible to prepare for the speaking test?

口试部分可能事先准备吗?

Yes. The more you learn about and understand the test, the more confident and less nervous you will feel. *IELTS Superior Speaking* will teach you exactly how to prepare for each section.

可以。越了解这个考试，你就越有信心，同时可以减轻压力。本书会指导你准备好每一部分的口语考试。

2. Are there any shortcuts to getting a high score?

有任何捷径可以帮助我拿到高分吗?

Unfortunately not. However, *IELTS Superior Speaking* will teach you how to maximise your score. How quickly you improve all depends on how much time and effort you can afford to allocate to preparing for the test.

很遗憾，没有。不过，本书可以帮助你提高分数，至于多快可以有进步，则完全取决于你花了多少时间与心思准备这个考试。

3. How quickly can I expect to improve 1 band?

进步 1 分需要花多久的时间?

All linguistic theory books suggest it takes around 200 hours of learning and practice to improve 1 level. However this may be reduced for those students who may have been out of practice with English for some time and are just trying to regain their former glory. And some students have a natural gift for learning languages.

依语言学习的理论来看，至少需要花 200 个小时学习才会进步 1 分。但有些人只是过去一段时间疏于学习，而有些人具有语言天分，对他们来说，进步 1 分所需的时间可能较短。

4. Is it best to have a British examiner as a teacher?

如果找英国籍口试官当老师会比较好吗?

Your teacher doesn't need to be an examiner nor British. They just need to have a thorough understanding of the IELTS and be qualified and experienced to teach you the skills and strategies of the IELTS.

你的老师不需要是口试官或英国人，只要他们了解 IELTS 的测试方式，并且具备指导 IELTS 的专业能力与经验即可。

5. How can I improve my speaking?

如何提高我的口试能力?

Practice, Practice, Practice. The more you practice, the more you will learn, which leads to higher confidence and lower nerves.

练习、练习、再练习! 你练习得越多，就会越有自信。

6. Should I find a speaking partner?

我需要找一个可以跟我练习对话的人吗?

Yes. Otherwise how can you practice? It doesn't need to be a foreigner nor do you need to get a foreign boyfriend/girlfriend. Your partner could be a fellow Chinese who is preparing for IELTS or just wants to improve his/her English also.

这是必要的。不过你不需要因此而找外国人来作为你练习英语的对象，你的练习对象可以是正在准备 IELTS 考试的考生，或是想提高英文能力的人。

The Candidate's Guide to An Examiner's Marking Criteria
口试评分标准——考生要诀

Criterion 评分标准	Do 一定要	Don't 千万不可
Fluency and Coherence 流畅性及连贯性	■ Speak at a steady, constant speed 说话速度适中 ■ Speak naturally without noticeable effort 说话自然不做作 ■ Give extended answers 给出具延伸性的答案 ■ Develop your opinions 拓展你的想法、意见 ■ Use linking devices to organise your ideas logically 适当使用连词及转折语	■ Repeat yourself 重复叙述 ■ Self correct yourself too much 过多自我纠正 ■ Speak slowly 说话太慢 ■ Pause, hesitate or break down 停顿、迟疑或突然不知所措 ■ Overuse linking devices 过度使用连词和转折语 ■ Jump around between ideas 跳跃式思考、说法不连贯
Lexical Resource 词汇量	■ Use sophisticated vocabulary 使用较难但贴切的词汇 **原句**：MRT system is very good. **建议**：MRT system is very effective. ■ Demonstrate specialised terminology 必要时，使用专有名词或术语 ■ Produce less common expressions 尽量少用老生常谈的用语 ■ Add some idiomatic language 使用一些谚语 ■ Use the correct word forms and collocations 使用正确的词性与搭配 ■ Produce the vocabulary in appropriate situations 依情景、前后文，选择适当词汇	■ Rely on mime or gestures to convey meaning 用表情、动作或手势来表达想法 ■ Repeat vocabulary whenever possible 重复已说过的词汇 ■ Think of the easiest word to express something but also avoid taking too many risks with complex vocabulary in the interests of maintaining coherence 为了达到连贯而选择使用非常简单的词汇，并刻意不使用较复杂、较难的词汇

Grammatical Range and Accuracy 语法运用范围及其正确性	■ Use a wide range of both simple and complex structures 同时运用简单及复杂的语法结构 ■ Demonstrate flexible use of structures 融汇运用不同的语法结构 ■ Focus on accuracy without losing fluency 语法运用要确切且流利 ■ Be communicative 畅所欲言	■ Produce too many errors 犯太多错误 ■ Use structures repetitively 不断重复使用相同的语法结构 ■ Demonstrate only short sentence forms 仅用短句表达
Pronunciation 发音	■ Try and reduce your accent 尽量减少你的口音 ■ Articulate words 口齿清晰 ■ Contract words where possible 使用“缩略语” **原句：** I will be there. **建议：** I'll be there. ■ Use weakened forms 使用“弱读音” **原句：** salt and pepper **建议：** salt “n” pepper ■ Demonstrate an ability of sound links 使用“连音” **原句：** it's a **建议：** it's a ■ Use the correct word and sentence stress 正确发出单词及句子的“重音” ■ Speak with the correct rhythm and intonation 说话要抑扬顿挫	■ Articulate each word separately 将相关的词汇分开或间断地说 ■ Speak in monotone 音调单调没有起伏 ■ Cause strain or confusion to the listener 造成听者的紧张或困惑

NB

When looking at the marking criteria it is worth noting that each criterion is equally weighted so try to strike a balance between the 4 criteria.

Sample IELTS Interviews

Listen to the following recordings to hear the difference between an IELTS band 4.5, 5, 6, 7.5 and 9. Comments have been provided on each of the students' performances according to the above criteria.

请听录音——IELTS 口试成绩 4.5 分、5 分、6 分、7.5 分和 9 分的模拟示范，并找出其差异性。另外请参考“口试评分标准(FC，LR，GRA，P)”来解读 4 位示范学生表现的评分表。

Possible IELTS Band 4.5
4.5 分(参考分数)

Part 1 *Track 09*

Hello, my name is (examiner's name).
What's your full name please?
And your Chinese name?
What can I call you?
Can I check your ID and passport please?
In the first part, I'd like to ask you some general questions about yourself.

Let's talk about your job or studies.
- What do you do?
- Describe a typical day in your job.
- What's the most difficult thing about your job?
- What have you learnt from your boss?

Now I'd like to ask you about memories.
- Do you like to think about the past? *Why/Why not?*
- What are some ways that you remember the past?
- What is one of your favourite memories?

Let's move on to pets.
- Have you ever had a pet?
- Which pets are popular in your country?
- Why do people enjoy pets?

Part 2

In Part 2, I will give you a topic and I'd like you to talk about it for 1-2 minutes. Before you talk, you will have one minute to think about what you are going to say. You may make some notes if you wish. Do you understand?

Topic Card

Describe a relaxing activity.
You should say:
- what it is
- where you do it
- how it relaxes you

and explain why you enjoy it.

- How did you find out about this activity?
- Would other people find this relaxing?

Part 3

You've been talking about a relaxing activity and I'd like to ask you one or two more questions related to this. Let's consider first of all:

The importance of relaxation
- Describe how important it is to lead a balanced life.
- Compare how people relaxed in the past to more modern relaxation techniques.
- Explain what dangers there are of no relaxation time.

Stress
- Suggest some positive and negative ways people deal with stress.
- *Agree/Disagree* that children's lives are more stressful than before.

Thank you. That is the end of the speaking test.

NB

The scores are given as a guide only and may not be a true indication of what the student would get in the official test. The following is an examiner's comments, which should be used so that you can learn from other people's mistakes and not to determine your score.
（以下分数仅供参考，评分表可以给考生提供从他人的错误中学习的机会。）

Kender

Criterion 评分标准	Mistake 错误	Example 举例说明	Correction/Advice 指正与建议
FC 流畅性及连贯性 **4** 分	Unable to extend 回答得太少	A number of questions in Part 1 were answered with only 1 sentence.	Try to say at least 3 sentences for each answer in Part 1.
	Short responses 回答得太短	Part 2 just over 1 minute	It's better to speak closer to 2 minutes than 1 minute.
	Slow to respond 反应得太慢	Kender couldn't understand the first & second questions in Part 3 so remained silent.	If you don't understand, then you may ask the examiner to explain in Part 3. If you remain silent you get no points in each criterion.
	Slow speech 讲得太慢	The pace throughout the interview was too slow.	Try to speak at a steady, constant speed.
LR 词汇量 **4** 分	Inappropriate vocab. 不恰当的用词	➤ Inside activities	➤ Indoor activities
	Wrong collocations 错误的搭配	➤ Do a little trouble	➤ Have a little trouble
	Wrong prepositions 介词的误用	➤ In the weekend	➤ *At*/*On* the weekend
	Repetitive vocabulary 重复的词汇	"Maybe" was repeated at least 5 times.	There are many different ways to say "maybe", see page 115.
	Simple vocabulary 过于简单的词汇	Throughout the interview there was no use of complex vocabulary.	Don't always think of the easiest way of answering a question, try to show more sophistication.

Criterion 评分标准	Mistake 错误	Example 举例说明	Correction/Advice 指正与建议
GRA 语法运用范围与其正确性 **4**分	Wrong word order 词序错误	➤ My boss is good emotion control.	➤ He controls his emotions well.
	Wrong modals 错误的语态	➤ I will working	➤ I will work
	Wrong tenses 错误的时态	➤ Before I teaching	➤ Before I teach
	Simple structures 过于简单的语法结构	Throughout the interview the most complex structures were clauses connected with "and", "so", "because", "but".	Remember there are so many ways to express "and", "so", "because", "but". Every student knows these structures. Be more sophisticated.
P 发音 **6**分	No contractions 没有使用"缩略语"	➤ I will working	➤ I'll work
	Incomplete sounds 发音不完整	➤ Physics	➤ Physics [ˈfɪzɪks]
		➤ Dangerous	➤ Dangerous [ˈdeɪndʒərəs]
	Wrong sounds 错误的发音	➤ Experiment [iː]	➤ Experiment [e]
		➤ Walk vs Work	➤ Walk [ɔː] ; Work [ɜː]
		➤ Instrument [iː]	➤ Instrument [ɪ]
	Chinese English 中式发音	➤ Is [ɪzə]	➤ Is [ɪz]
		➤ But [bʌtə]	➤ But [bʌt]

Possible IELTS Band 5
5 分(参考分数)

Part 1 *Track 10*

Hello, my name is (examiner's name).
What's your full name please?
What can I call you?
Can I check your ID and passport please?
In the first part, I'd like to ask you some general questions about yourself.

Let's talk about your work or school.

- Are you a student or do you work?
- How do you travel to work?
- What training did you need for this job?
- Are there any other jobs you would like to do in the future?

Now I'd like to discuss sport.

- Which sports are you good at?
- Which sport do you think is the most dangerous?
- Which famous sports person would you like to meet? Why?

Let's move on to clothes and fashion.

- What kind of clothes do you feel comfortable in?
- Are brand names important to you?
- Do you often buy new clothes?

Part 2

In Part 2, I will give you a topic and I'd like you to talk about it for 1-2 minutes. Before you talk, you will have one minute to think about what you are going to say. You may make some notes if you wish. Do you understand?

Topic Card

Describe an unhealthy habit you have.
You should say:
- what it is
- when and how often you do it
- why it is unhealthy

and explain what you can do about it.

- Do you think it will get more serious?

Part 3

You've been talking about an unhealthy activity and I'd like to ask you one or two more questions related to this. Let's consider first of all:

Health
- Comment on how much healthcare support your government provides.
- Compare how healthy people are today to the past.

Medicine
- Compare the benefits of western medicine to natural medicine.
- Assess how dependent we are on medicine these days.

Thank you. That is the end of the speaking test.

Shang

Criterion 评分标准	Mistake 错误	Example 举例说明	Correction/Advice 指正与建议
FC 流畅性及连贯性 5分	Slow speech 讲得太慢	Shang relied on slow speech throughout the interview to keep talking.	Remember if you speak slowly the examiner will hear every mistake. At a more steady speed some mistakes may be missed. Although grammatical accuracy was high, a balance must be struck with fluency.
	Pauses 停顿太多	Pauses often occurred before the use of more complex vocabulary or grammar.	If you can't think of how to say a word, then try to paraphrase. Balance complexity with fluency.
	Unable to extend 讲得太少	Most answers in Part 1 were 1-2 sentences.	Try to say at least 3 sentences for each question in Part 1.
LR 词汇量 4分	Inappropriate vocab. 不恰当的用词	➤ If I was in an emergency case	➤ If I was/were (informal/formal) in an emergency *Or* In case of an emergency
		➤ At first time	➤ At first
		➤ I ask for my dentist	➤ I asked my dentist
		➤ Lessen this kind of syndrome	➤ Lessen the effect of this kind of syndrome
	Missing prepositions 缺少介词	➤ Abrasion your enamel	➤ Abrasions to your enamel
GRA 语法运用范围与其正确性 5分	Missing articles 缺少冠词	➤ I take MRT	➤ I take the MRT
	Missing verbs 缺少动词	➤ The driver always in a very high speed state.	➤ The driver always goes at a very high speed.
	Passive vs Active 被动与主动	➤ Let me wear on my teeth.	➤ It is worn on my teeth.
	Wrong word order 词序错误	➤ Prevent my teeth from abrasion.	➤ Prevent abrasions to my teeth.

Criterion 评分标准	Mistake 错误	Example 举例说明	Correction/Advice 指正与建议
	Incorrect subject-verb agreement 主语与动词不一致	➤ Modern people is healthier.	➤ Modern people are healthier.
	Inappropriate tenses 错误的时态	➤ People in the past don't have so much pressure.	➤ People in the past didn't have so much pressure.
P 发音 6分	Wrong sound 错误的发音	➤ State, make, strange, famous [æ]	➤ State, make, strange, famous [eɪ]
		➤ Pyjamas [ɑːz]	➤ Pyjamas [əz]
		➤ Grind [ɑː]	➤ Grind [aɪ]
	Wrong stress 重音错误	➤ Painkíller	➤ Páinkiller

Possible IELTS Band 6
6 分(参考分数)

Part 1 *Track 11*

Hello, my name is (examiner's name).
What's your full name please?
What can I call you?
Can I check your ID and passport please?
In the first part, I'd like to ask you some general questions about yourself.

Let's talk about your hometown.
- Where are you from?
- What is the area like where you live?
- Is there anything you would like to change about your hometown?

Now I'd like to talk about your family. Is that okay?
- Do you have a large or small family?
- When do you get together as a family?
- What do you like to do with your family?

Let's move on to your free time.
- Do you have a lot of free time?
- How do you spend your time away from work or studies?
- Do you prefer to spend time alone or with friends? Why?

Part 2

In Part 2, I will give you a topic and I'd like you to talk about it for 1-2 minutes. Before you talk, you will have one minute to think about what you are going to say. You may make some notes if you wish. Do you understand?

Topic Card

> Describe something that you would love to learn.
> You should say:
> ■ what it is
> ■ how you will learn it
> ■ what it may lead to in the future
> and explain why you are interested in it.

■ Do you think you will be good at it?

Part 3

You've been talking about something you would like to learn and I'd like to ask you one or two more questions related to this. Let's consider first of all:

Education

■ Explain how the education system in your country has changed over the past 50 years.
■ Suggest some changes the Education Department should make in your country to the education system.

Schools

■ Compare the effectiveness of coeducational and single sex schools.
■ *Agree/Disagree* that exams are the best way to measure what a student has learnt.
■ Consider who you learn more from—your teachers or your parents?
■ Predict how education and learning will change in the future.

Thank you. That is the end of the speaking test.

Steven

Criterion 评分标准	Mistake 错误	Example 举例说明	Correction/Advice 指正与建议
FC 流畅性及连贯性 6 分	Misunderstood questions 误解问题	When do you get together as a family?	If you don't understand a question in Part 1, you may ask the examiner to repeat but not to explain. In Part 2 you may ask the examiner to explain the topic card (Steven described something he has learnt, not something he would love to learn in the future).
		Describe something you would love to learn.	
	Short responses in Part 1 回答得太短	➤ I have a small family. ➤ I do have a lot of free time.	Try to say at least 3 sentences for Part 1 questions.
	Slower speech and hesitations in Part 3 讲得太慢、停顿太多	Pauses before more complex vocabulary and grammar in Part 3	Try to speak without noticeable effort in all parts of the interview.
LR 词汇量 6 分	Chinese English 中式英语	➤ Do you understand? → Understand.	➤ Do you understand? → Yes, I do.
	Inappropriate vocab. 不恰当的用词	➤ The reason I like it because...	➤ The reason I like it is...
		➤ As what I mentioned...	➤ As I mentioned...
		➤ Daily speaking English	➤ Everyday English
		➤ We stand the frontier	➤ We are in the frontline
		➤ Cosex	➤ Coed
	Word forms 不恰当的用法	➤ Delicate food	➤ Delicacies
		➤ Makes my feelings better	➤ Makes me feel better
		➤ Share some gossips (n.)	➤ Gossip (v.)

Criterion 评分标准	Mistake 错误	Example 举例说明	Correction/Advice 指正与建议
GRA 语法运用范围与其正确性 **5** 分	Countable vs Uncountable 可数与不可数名词	➤ A lot of pleasures	➤ A lot of pleasure
		➤ Other entertainments	➤ Other forms of entertainment
	Incorrect subject-verb agreement 主语与动词不一致	➤ Taipei have...	➤ Taipei has...
	Wrong modals 错误的语态	➤ Taipei should need...	➤ Taipei should... Taipei needs...
	Comparatives 比较级	➤ More faster	➤ Faster
	Wrong word order 词序错误	➤ It makes us easier to...	➤ It makes it easier for us to...
		➤ Instead of what your neighbours is happening...	➤ Instead of what is happening with your neighbours...
	Indirect speech 间接表述	➤ Global view of what the world is going.	➤ Global view of where the world is going.
P 发音 **6** 分	Unnecessary sounds 多余的发音	➤ Portfolio [pɔːtəˈfəʊliəʊ]	➤ Portfolio [pɔːtˈfəʊliəʊ]

Possible IELTS Band 7.5
7.5 分(参考分数)

Part 1 *Track 12*

Hello, my name is (examiner's name).
What's your full name please?
What can I call you?
Can I check your ID and passport please?
In the first part, I'd like to ask you some general questions about yourself.

Let's talk about what you do.
- Do you work or are you a student?
- Why did you choose this job?
- Is your company a good one? Why/Why not?
- When would you like to retire?

Now I'd like you to speak about art.
- How often do you visit a museum or art gallery?
- Did you learn Art at high school?
- Are there any famous artists from your country?

Let's discuss transport.
- What kinds of public transport are available in your city?
- Why do people take public transport instead of private transport like cars or motorcycles?
- Should public transport be made cheaper?

Part 2

In Part 2, I will give you a topic and I'd like you to talk about it for 1-2 minutes. Before you talk, you will have one minute to think about what you are going to say. You may make some notes if you wish. Do you understand?

Topic Card

Describe an electronic device you own.
You should say:
- what it is
- what it looks like
- what functions it has

and explain why you like it.

- Would you recommend this product to others?

Part 3

You've been talking about an electronic device that you own and I'd like to ask you one or two more questions related to this. Let's consider first of all:

The Internet
- Is Internet banking popular in your country?
- Suggest some ways to make the Internet safer for children to use.

Information technology
- Justify the amount of money spent worldwide developing technology.
- Speculate on how technology will develop in the future.

Thank you. That is the end of the speaking test.

Haley

Criterion 评分标准	Mistake 错误	Example 举例说明	Correction/Advice 指正与建议
FC 流畅性及连贯性 7分	Short responses in Parts 1 & 2 回答得太短	A number of answers consisted of only 1 sentence. The examiner had asked all questions within 3 minutes in Part 1. Part 2 was just under 90 seconds.	Try to say at least 3 sentences for each question in Part 1. Try to speak for closer to 2 minutes than 1 in part.
LR 词汇量 7分	Inappropriate vocabulary 不恰当的用词	➤ I can't complain more.	➤ I can't complain at all.
		➤ I am still young though.	➤ As I'm still young.
		➤ Maybe put in the pocket.	➤ Maybe fits in the pocket.
		➤ What we have now and back 10 years...	➤ What we have now compared to 10 years ago...
	Missing/inappropriate/extra prepositions 介词的误用	➤ Apply it online	➤ Apply for it online
		➤ How to get sources they want?	➤ How to get to the sources they want?
		➤ Technology is what we can't live without with.	➤ Technology is what we can't live without.
		➤ In the corner	➤ On the corner
GRA 语法运用范围与其正确性 8分	Wrong tenses 错误的时态	➤ That's why I choose this job.	➤ That's why I chose this job.
	Countable vs Uncountable 可数与不可数名词	➤ MRTs	➤ The MRT
	Wrong word order 词序错误	➤ It's too much expensive.	➤ It's much too expensive.
	Wrong modals 错误的语态	➤ I just wouldn't imagine...	➤ I just couldn't imagine...
	Incorrect subject-verb agreement 主语与动词不一致	➤ Whatever teachers says...	➤ Whatever teachers say...
P 发音 8分	Haley's pronunciation is clear and natural at all times.		

Possible IELTS Band 9
9 分(参考分数)

Part 1 *Track 13*

Hello, my name is (examiner's name).
What's your full name please?
Can I check your ID and passport please?
In the first part, I'd like to ask you some general questions about yourself.

Let's talk about where you are from.
- Where's your hometown?
- Which places should tourists visit?
- Is there anything you don't like about your hometown?

Let's move on to the weather.
- What is the weather like where you live?
- Do you prefer summer or winter?
- What do you like to do when it's raining?

Now I'd like to ask some questions about shopping.
- Who do you like to go shopping with?
- Do you prefer shopping malls or traditional markets?

Part 2

In part 2, I will give you a topic and I'd like you to talk about it for 1-2 minutes. Before you talk, you will have one minute to think about what you are going to say. You may make some notes if you wish. Do you understand?

Topic Card

> Describe someone famous that you admire.
> You should say:
> ■ who the person is
> ■ what they do
> ■ how they became successful
> and explain why you admire them.

Part 3

You've been talking about someone famous that you admire and I'd like to ask you one or two more questions related to this. Let's consider first of all:

Fame
- Evaluate the pros and cons of being famous.
- Explain what responsibilities celebrities have to our society.

Success
- Discuss which element is more important for success: luck or hard work?
- Define how success is measured.
- Describe how success can change a person.

Thank you. That is the end of the speaking test.

Petula

SCRIPT 对话内容

The following scripts are of native speakers and are totally unedited so you will find there are some grammatical errors. Even native speakers will make some grammatical errors. Those mistakes which are similar to native speakers are not penalised by the examiner.
以下对话中的考生是母语为英语的外国人，且其对话完全未经修改，所以你仍可发现有些语法上的错误。这告诉我们即使是母语为英语的人讲英语时也会犯错。如果你也犯了类似的错误，那么这些错误并不会被口试官扣分。

Part 1

Hello, my name is Christopher. What's your full name please?

My full name is Petula Parris.

Can I check your ID and passport please?

Yeah sure.

That's fine. Thank you. Now in the first part, I'd like to ask you some general questions about yourself. Let's talk about where you are from.

OK.

Where's your hometown?

My hometown is in the south west of England. The south west of England is all countryside so I live in the countryside on a farm, in a, it's not actually a village it's just a farm by itself in a valley so we don't have any neighbours. It's just all of our, all of our fields and then not far from our farm is the coast.

OK, and which places should tourists visit?

Well, there's lots of places tourists can visit actually. We even have lots of tourists staying in our farmhouse and they can walk around the countryside.

There's lots of different country walks or hiking coz there's lots of forests and then you can go to the coast, to the seaside. There's a small seaside town there so there's lots of different kinds of souvenir shops and restaurants and cafes, some swimming pools or you can swim in the sea if it's not too cold. There's lots of coastal walks or there's lots of coastal paths that you could cycle along so it's those kinds of things just walking, cycling, being kind of outdoor activities.

And is there anything you don't like about your hometown?

I think probably the biggest problem is that it's a bit boring sometimes, like I said there's no neighbours and even the seaside village we live near is really quite, really quite small. So apart from the summer there's not really anyone there. In the winter it's really quiet so there's not much to do when you're young.

OK, let's move on to the weather. What is the weather like where you live?

Well the summer's quite nice. It's usually quite sunny and hot in the summer. The winter's cold. It rains a lot. Sometimes it snows but when it snows, the snow doesn't really settle very much, it's never very deep and then the autumn and the winter. The autumn's quite cold as well actually. You can't really differentiate the autumn from the winter and then the spring that's quite cold as well, yeah.

OK, so do you prefer summer or winter?

I definitely prefer the summer because there's not very much sun in the winter and I think when there's no sun it's really depressing. When there's sun you can do loads of things—you can go to the beach, you can go outside, you can do sport, you can just do anything without worrying about being cold. So I like the summer definitely.

And what do you like to do when it's raining?

Well it does rain quite a lot of, it does rain quite a lot of the time in England so I usually go to an indoor swimming pool or go to the cinema or just stay at home and read, watch TV. I mean if you have an umbrella, you can still go outside and go walking anyway.

OK, now I'd like to ask you some questions about shopping. Who do you like to go shopping with?

Well really I only like going by myself. I really hate going with other people because it takes ages to walk around with them because sometimes they want to go to different shops than you do and if they want to try on clothes, you have to wait for them or if you want to try on clothes, they have to wait for you. And I don't really like having to listen to what they think about the clothes I'm trying so I just like going by myself.

And do you prefer shopping malls or markets?

I definitely prefer shopping malls coz if you go to traditional markets, then often you can't try the clothes on. Although it's cheaper, the quality isn't always very good so if you can't try it on, you don't know if it fits and then if you, when you've gone home and you try it on, it doesn't fit, you can't usually take it back to markets but in shopping malls if there's a problem you can take it back, you just need a receipt. They have changing rooms. You can try it on so I think that's much better.

<u>Part 2</u>

OK. (*cough*) Sorry. Let's move on to Part 2. I will give you a topic and I'd like you to talk about it for 1-2 minutes. Before you talk, you will have one minute to think about what you are going to say. You may make some notes if you wish. Do you understand?

Yes.

OK, so here's your paper and a pen and here's your topic. I'd like you to describe someone famous that you admire.

OK. I'd like to talk about a man called Nelson Mandela. I'm sure you know who he is. He's very famous around the whole world because he used to be the president of South Africa. Now I admire him not because he was the president but because he fought throughout his whole life. I mean, he's already an old man, possibly 80 I think, and he fought throughout his whole life for something he believed in. He really stuck to his guns. He followed what he believed in, stuck to his principles which were, what he fought for was racial equality in South Africa during apartheid. He wanted equality between black and white people and I mean his life was very difficult he was imprisoned for 40 years. Even before he was imprisoned, he was always wanted by the South African government and despite all this, he still never gave up what he believed in. Even when he was in jail he found lots of ways of continuing the struggle whether it was through other prisoners; He, he also passed communications and kept the movement going through some of the prison wardens that, that sympathised with him and his cause. So despite being in prison for 40 years, he still could, he, he could still fight for what he thought was right and I mean, in our everyday lives, we meet lots of things that we want to give up on. Even if it's just an exam or something like that so I really can't imagine how difficult it must be to fight for the same thing for your whole life and not give up.

Part 3

OK. Let's move on to Part 3. You've been talking about someone famous that you admire and I'd like to ask you one or two more questions related to this. Let's consider first of all fame. Could you please evaluate the pros and cons of being famous?

I think, I think there's probably more disadvantages to being famous than advantages. The obvious advantages are money. I mean, when you're famous, everybody wants you to do things; be on adverts, do speeches, just loads of things so you earn lots of money. And if you have lots of money, you can just, you can just do anything you want and you get to meet, you get loads of opportunities. You get to meet lots of people that you wouldn't have met; lots of, do lots of things that you wouldn't have been able to do. You get special treatment. You can go to parties like really like the Oscars and things like that. But because most famous people are really in the public eye all of the time, there's a huge pressure on your personal life. People want to know about your family and your relationships and everything you do so there's really an invasion of privacy by the media. I think that's a really big disadvantage. You can't, you can't just, you can't just live normally anymore you really have to adapt to being a public figure. I think that's a big disadvantage.

OK. And can you please explain what responsibilities celebrities have to our society?

Well, I think because it's society that makes the celebrity famous, I don't really think the celebrities have any responsibilities to society. I think society, because society is responsible for making the celebrity famous then if they think the celebrity is doing anything wrong then it's up to society to not support them anymore or show that, that they disapprove of what they are doing. So I really think it's, I think society has more responsibility than the celebrity.

OK. And let's talk about success. Could you discuss which element is more important for success: luck or hard work?

Well, we say in English ... What's the saying? ... "If at first you don't succeed, try, try again" and I think that displays that really, really hard work is a big element of being successful. But then you also need to "speculate to accumulate" and if you speculate, you're taking risks and if you take risks, I think you really need luck to be on your side. So you definitely need a certain, a certain element of, of good luck. You need to be in the right place in the right time and meet the right people and if you're, you're, if you have a business, then you need the economy to be favourable or the market to be favourable so I think probably more hard luck ... ah hard luck!?! More hard work but a little bit of luck is definitely needed to get started.

OK. And could you define how success can be measured?

I think it's probably usually measured in money. Often when we say the most successful people, we mean the people with most money but then it can also be measured in status like your social position like we think presidents are successful, important politicians are successful. I suppose you could also measure it, you could measure it in how happy, happy the people are but I don't think people really use that kind of measurement. I think definitely, definitely money would be the main, the main way to measure success.

OK, and could you describe how success can change a person?

Well, I think that when people, when people are successful sometimes they, coz they've achieved what they've wanted to achieve they kind of lose all interest so they just want to be more successful or they feel a bit depressed because they don't know what the point of living is anymore. I remember I watched a film recently called *Alexander* and he was just a very successful warrior and he conquered country after country but each time he succeeded in conquering a new country, then he was bored again so he had to conquer another country. So sometimes I think it means that you kind of, you kind of lose your interest in life and you don't know what the point of living is anymore. And then obviously if it, if success comes with fame, then you have to adapt to being famous and that sometimes makes your life, you have to be quite distant from your family and friends. You don't know who you can trust anymore. If they'll sell, if they'll, you don't know if they'll sell your story to the papers or, or tell your secrets to people so you probably have to make a lot of adaptions in your, in your private life.

OK. Thank you. That is the end of the speaking test.

DIY Study Guide for Speaking
口语能力——自学要诀

Fluency & Coherence
流畅性及连贯性

1. Repeat after a recording
复述练习

The first time you repeat it will probably be slower than the actual recording so keep repeating until you gain the same speed as the native speaker. Be aware that you may need to use sound links, contractions and weakened forms to match their speed.

通常第一次做复述练习时，说的速度会比较慢，你必须重复练习，直到你讲话的速度与以英语为母语的使用者的速度一致。练习速度时你必须同时活用“连音”、“缩略语”以及“弱读音”。

2. Repeat the same topic
重复练习相同的主题

The first time you say a Part 2 topic, for example, you will produce a somewhat slow response with little information. The more often you repeat it, the more fluently your response should come out. Remember when you begin to produce more fluent answers, you will need to add more information to ensure that you keep talking for 1-2 minutes.

刚开始练习口语测试的 Part 2 时，你的反应会较慢，头脑中的资料会比较少，重复练习可以改善这种状况。记住，当你讲得比较流利后，你就必须提供充分的资料来让你的回答足以持续 1～2 分钟。

3. Use it or lose it
尽可能使用新词汇

The reason why you pause or hesitate is often in search of vocabulary which is not readily available to you. The more you use a word, the more likely it will become active vocabulary. By the same token if you never use a word that you have learnt, it is destined to be forgotten.

通常你在口试时停顿或犹豫，是因为你正在脑海里寻找合适的词汇。平时多练习使用学过的词汇，词汇才会真正属于你。

4. Focus on English, not IQ

专注在英文能力上

Another reason why you may break down is that you have no opinion. As a student about to study your Master's Degree, of course you want to sound very educated and knowledgeable, but remember IELTS stands for International English Language Testing System, it's not an IQ test. Examiners are testing your English not your intelligence. If you can't think of a smart response, then say something obvious, boring, or even stupid but use good English while you are doing so. Saying something is better than nothing. If you say nothing then you lose points in each criterion, not just fluency. If you say something stupid, you will still gain points in each criterion. The only thing you may lose is face but who cares? You'll never see the examiner again.

导致你在发言中停顿的另一个原因是因为你没有自己的看法。参加 IELTS 测试的考生多半是为了攻读硕士，当然会希望自己听起来是个有知识的人。但请牢记，IELTS 考查的是你的英文能力，而非智力。如果实在没有好的想法，或只有一些无趣、甚至愚蠢的想法，还是要尽量开口说，因为随便说也比什么都不说好。

5. Read, read, read

阅读各类型的文章

Again if you break down due to a lack of opinions then start reading up on a variety of topics and pay particular attention to different people's opinions. Nobody ever has a totally original opinion—everyone copies and adapts a number of ideas from various people when formulating their own opinion.

如果你是因为缺乏想法而导致回答停顿的话，那你必须开始阅读各种类型的文章，并多注意别人所发表的意见。没有人天生就是文思泉涌的，每个人都是参考别人的各种想法并将其转换成自己的意见。

6. Don't be shy for 11-14 minutes

暂时抛开害羞的个性

Even if you are shy in your native country using your native language—a person known to be of few words, you will have to change your personality for a mere 11-14 minutes as the examiner can only make an evaluation of what he/she hears. Again, if they hear nothing or very little, then it will affect each criterion. Try to be as talkative as possible and say as much as possible.

如果你是个害羞或不善言辞的人，那你必须在口试的 11～14 分钟里暂时抛开你害羞的个性，尽可能让自己表现得像个能言善辩的人。

7. Use signpost expressions

使用“指引性”的词语

Signpost expressions are words that give the listener some direction, for example: Firstly, By this I mean, For instance, In contrast, To be honest. All these expressions give the listener some idea of what kind of information to expect next, which makes it easier to follow and understand the conversation.

使用一些“指引性”的词语，给听者指引方向，让听者能立即且清楚地知道你要表达的信息，例如：Firstly （首先）、By this I mean（我的意思是）、For instance（例如）、In contrast（相反）、To be honest（老实说）。

Lexical Resource
词汇量

1. Read, read, read
尽可能多地阅读文章

Read something you enjoy reading; the more you enjoy it, the more you will read and the more you read, the more vocabulary you will learn. It doesn't matter if you are reading a signpost on the street or *Harry Potter*—you can learn English anywhere and everywhere.

读一些你感兴趣的文章或书籍，读得越多，你学习到的词汇就越多。不管是街上的标语，还是像《哈利·波特》这样的小说，英文的学习是无所不在的。

2. Review, review, review
复习，复习，再复习

If you don't review, you will forget. It is often boring to review, but it is absolutely essential to retain and consolidate vocabulary learnt. There's no point learning new words, in fact it would be a waste of time if you can't even remember the words you have learnt previously.

如果你不花时间复习，是很容易忘记的。复习虽然很无趣，但这是记住并巩固词汇必要的方法。如果连已经学过的词汇都记不得，那么拼命学新词汇也只是在浪费时间。

3. Use an English-English dictionary
使用英-英字典

It may be difficult at first but it will have far-reaching effects, as every time you learn a new word you will be reviewing old vocabulary. These days learner dictionaries only use around 2,000 of the most common words found in the English language. Such a vocabulary base should already be developed by the stage a student gets to high school. A translator may have short-term benefits but will only slow you down in the long run.

一开始用英-英字典会感到困难，但当你使用它查询新词汇时，你会同时复习到旧的词汇，这样的学习最有效。一般的英-英字典约使用 2000 个一般性词汇，而这些词汇是学生在高中阶段就已具备的。使用电子字典，虽然可以快速查到词汇的意思，但就长远来看，这反而会减慢你的学习脚步。

4. Use it or lose it
尽可能使用新词汇

Always try to use new words in conversation or writing as this is the best way to remember a word. The more you use it, the easier it will be to recall next time you wish to use it.

当你学习一个新单词后，最好的办法是一有机会就使用它。

5. Practise paraphrasing
练习改述

As a non-native speaker, it doesn't matter how many words you learn; there will always be a time when you don't know the word for something you wish to express. This will be even more likely when you are in a test and you are feeling nervous, tired and maybe even scared. Therefore it's important that you have the ability to paraphrase. Open up any book or even a dictionary and see if you can describe a word using other words—you may use a synonym, parallel expression or even a sentence to describe your meaning. Even native speakers use this technique as everyone's mind goes blank from time to time.

对于母语非英语的人来说，不论你学了多少单词，仍然会有词穷的时候，尤其在考试太过紧张时。因此，具备使用不同的表达方式来表达临时想不出的词汇的能力是极重要的。从一本书或字典中随意选一个词，试着使用同义词甚至是句子来表达它的意思。就连母语为英语的人在临时找不到词汇表达时，也会如法炮制。

6. Learn all word forms

学习所有的词性变化

Students most commonly use an incorrect word form, that is, they use a noun when they should use a verb or they use an adjective when they should use an adverb. When you learn a new word also find out what the part of speech is and what the other word forms are.

一般学生最常犯的错误就是词性，也就是该使用动词时却用了名词，或该用副词时却用了形容词。当你学到一个新的单词时，一定要把它的词性变化一起记下来。

Grammatical Range and Accuracy
语法运用范围与其正确性

1. Record yourself
录下自己的声音

Often when you are speaking you don't realise how many mistakes you make or what they are. You'll be surprised that you can actually pick up a lot of mistakes yourself if you replay your talk, and by copying it down, it will probably bring out even more errors. Once you've noted your most common errors, get yourself a grammar practice book and practise your weaknesses.

将自己的口试练习录下来，你会发现自己犯了许多平时没有发现的错误。记下自己最常犯的错误，并使用语法书来练习自己语法较弱的地方。

2. Take apart and reconstruct sentences
分解、重组句子结构

Open up any book and choose a sentence. Break up the sentence into smaller sentences and then without referring back to the original sentence see if you can put it back together again. In the IELTS you will need to be able to produce both short and complex sentence forms. You will not get a high score if you only use short simple sentences for the sake of accuracy.

随便从一本书中挑一个句子，练习将句子分解成几个较短的句子，再重组还原成完整的一句。在 IELTS 口试中，你必须兼顾短句及复合句的使用。如果为了句子的正确性而一直使用简短的句子，肯定是不会得到高分的。

3. Practise linking words and expressions
练习使用连词

The easiest way to make a sentence sound more complex is by using a linking word. Get yourself a grammar book and practise using conjunctions and linking words.

让一个句子听起来完整、漂亮的最简单方式就是使用连词，可使用语法书来练习连词的用法。

4. Read, read, read

持续阅读

The more you read, the more good grammar you will come across. The more accurate and complex grammar you are exposed to, the more likely it is that some of it will rub off on you.

你读得越多，就越能使用复杂而正确的语法，以此来精确地表达你的意思。

Pronunciation
发音

1. Note down phonemics

记下单词的音节

When you learn a new word, it is essential that you also learn how to say it otherwise you can use it in writing but not in speaking. By learning and using the phonemic script for each new word you learn, you will feel more confident when it comes to using it verbally.

当你学到一个新的单词时，练习它的正确发音是必要的，否则你充其量只会把词汇用在书写上而非口语上。

2. Repeat after a recording

复述练习

Practise repeating after a recording over and over again. The first time you may have the clarity but you will most likely be missing the other native speech patterns such as word and sentence stress, rhythm and intonation, sound links, weakened forms and contractions. Keep practising until it sounds identical to the native speaker.

做复述练习。你有可能已经说得很清楚，但却忽略了重音、音调或连音等。不断地练习，直到自己的发音能近似于母语为英语者。

3. Read aloud

大声念出来

This will help you to improve your motor skills. As English is not your mother tongue, your mouth will not be used to using certain muscles. Therefore they need to be given a workout as often as possible. If you read aloud a tapescript it will give you the opportunity also to listen and check your pronunciation.

这能帮助你训练嘴型和舌头。英语并非你的母语，所以你并不习惯于某些肌肉的运用，因此你必须时常练习。大声念出录音稿，你就有更多的机会检查自己的发音。

4. Listen, listen, listen

多听

The more you listen, the more familiar the sounds of the English language will become to you. This will assist in predicting the pronunciation of new words in case you do not have a dictionary handy to look up the phonemics.

多练习听力，你就能更熟悉英语音调，下次遇到新的词汇时，无须查字典也能发出正确的音。

IELTS

SUPERIOR SPEAKING

QPS 应考策略与实用笔记速记法

The QPS Strategy and Note-Making Skills

Speaking Test
Part 1

Part 1 of IELTS speaking is designed to warm you up and relax your nerves. Examiners will ask you general questions about yourself on topics that are familiar to all students. This section lasts for 4-5 minutes and includes a short introduction of the examiner and yourself, followed by a few questions on hometowns or jobs/studies and then a few more questions on other general topics.

口语测试的 Part 1 约 4～5 分钟，算是较为轻松的热身阶段。口试官会先问一些与你背景有关的问题，例如家乡、工作等等，接着再问一些一般性的问题。

QPS Strategy

QPS 应考策略

Identify the **Question**

↓

State a **Position**

↓

Offer **Support**

In this section of *IELTS Superior Speaking*, you will learn about the QPS strategy. You will be given a thorough listing of all the possible question types of Part 1. It is important that you immediately identify the type of Question so that you can decide how to respond appropriately. You should then state your Position, however this is not enough, as you must also provide some Support to the position you gave. So use the QPS strategy in order to help you give extended answers using sophisticated vocabulary and grammar. Remember you will not fare well in the test if you only give short responses.

本部分会提供口试 Part 1 可能会出现的问题。你必须快速地分析问题的类型并确认答题方向，然后提出有力的佐证。**QPS 应考策略**（问题—定位—支持）可以帮助你使用正确的语法和词汇，使回答更为完整。要记住，如果答案都很简短，是不会得到理想分数的。

Types of Questions and How to Answer Them
各类型问题及答题方式

Ability
能力

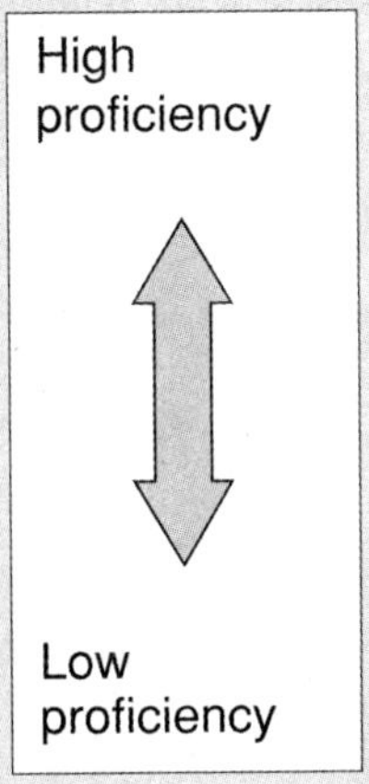

Examiner's Questions（主考官提问）

Question → Ability（能力）

- **Can you** cook?
- **Are you able to** cook?
- **Do you know how to** cook?
- **Are you capable of** cooking?
- **Are you good at** cooking?
- **How good are you at** cooking?

Student's Answers（考生回答）

Position → State level of proficiency（陈述该能力的程度）

- **I'm** ***an expert/a professional*** at cooking.
- **I can** cook **in my sleep.**
- **I have a knack for** cooking.
- **I'm a bit of a know-it-all when it comes to** cooking.
- Cooking **is one of my fortes.**

- **I can't** cook **to save my life.**
- **I can't** cook **for nuts.**
- **I don't know the first thing about** cooking.
- **I'm not much of** a chef.

Support → State reasons（陈述拥有该能力的缘由）

- **The reason why** I can cook so well **is** I'd watch and help my grandmother when she cooked up a storm in the family kitchen during my childhood.
- **The reason behind this is** the fact that my grandmother gave me a lot of secret family recipes.

- **The *chief/most compelling* reason is** I was forced to learn when I left home to study at university in another city.
- **The most obvious explanation is** when you're hungry and there's no one there to cook for you, coupled with the fact that you don't have enough money to eat out, well, then you learn pretty quickly.
- **I'd put it down to** my time in the military when I was assigned to cooking duties.
- **I'd attribute it to** the fact that I had very busy parents who, if they had to do overtime, would often ask me to prepare dinner for my younger brothers and sisters.
- **It's all thanks to** my Home Economics teacher who inspired me to forge a career as a chef.

NB

Every student in the interview will use "**because,**" so be careful not to overuse it. Show how wide your range of vocabulary and grammar is by not just learning one way to **state a reason**.

Comparing
比较

Examiner's Questions（主考官提问）

Question → Comparing （比较性的问题）

- **What are the (main)** ***differences/similarities*** **between** state **and** public schools?
- **How** ***is/are*** (a) state school(s) ***different from/similar to*** (a) public one(s)?
- **How are** state **and** public schools **alike**?

NB

In British English a public school is a private fee-paying school. A government-run institution is a state school. In Australian and North American English a private school is a fee-paying school and a public school is government-run.

Student's Answers（考生回答）

Position → Identify the *similarities/differences*
（区分相似性 / 相异处）

Total difference

- **They are like chalk and cheese**; public schools are only interested in making money while state-run schools focus on education.
- State schools **bear no relation to** public ones; state-run institutions only teach the bare minimum whereas public schools work the students to death.
- **There's a world of difference between** state **and** public schools, especially in regards to the quality and quantity of facilities that they have on offer.

Some *differences/ similarities*

- **One of the major** ***contrasts/distinguishing features*** **is** the teaching quality, as public schools usually attract teachers of higher calibre.
- **What sets** public **and** state schools **apart is** the tuition fees as state-run institutions are up to 10 times cheaper than their counterparts.
- **The most striking resemblance is** the course content as they both use exactly the same books and materials.

Exactly the same

- **I can't tell them apart**; teaching quality, course content, school grounds and facilities are all identical as far as I can tell.
- **I can't draw a distinction between** state **and** public schools; as far as I know they are identical in educational content and school facilities.

Support → Provide an example （举例）

- **A** ***classic/prime/fine/typical*** **example of this is** a public school called Wego.
- A public school called Wego **is a** ***classic/prime/fine/typical*** **example of this.**
- **Take** my high school which is state-run **for example**, we didn't even have a basketball court.
- **There's no better example than** the state-run primary school I attended.
- **In one case**, there was a public school which declared bankruptcy just after the new semester commenced and all tuition fees had been collected.
- **In some instances** public schools actually have a higher teacher to student ratio than state schools.
- **A case in point is** the newly opened public primary school in my area.
- There are many state schools which are just as popular as public schools…., **to name but a few.** (used when giving many examples)

NB

Every student in the interview will use "**the same**", "**different**", "**for example**", so be careful not to overuse them. Show how wide your range of vocabulary and grammar is by not just learning one way to **compare or give an example**.

Conditionals
有前提的提问

Examiner's Questions（主考官提问）

Question → Conditionals（有前提的提问）

- **What do you do if** you have a headache?
- **What will you do if** the weather's fine this weekend?
- **What would you do if** you lost your job?
- **What would you have done if** you hadn't gone to university?

Student's Answers（考生回答）

Position → State result (try and avoid repeating "if")
（说明结果，避免重复使用 if）

- **As long as** the sun's out, I'll go to the beach.
- **Provided that** there are no clouds about, I'll head off to the beach.
- **Unless** there's rain, I'll be making my way to the beach.
- **On condition that** it's not overcast, the beach will be my destination.
- **Supposing that** I was laid off, I'd head off to study overseas earlier than originally planned.
- **Say that** I no longer had a job, I'd probably bring forward my plans to study abroad.

Support 1 → Discuss the benefits（陈述优点）

- **The good thing about this is** I'll be able to improve my English sooner than expected.
- **The major advantage is** I may not have to wait until next year to begin my Master's Degree.
- **One of the *strengths/merits* is** I'll have more time to prepare before I depart.
- **On the plus side** I may make it over in time to attend a pre-sessional course.
- **The beauty of this is** I can have a short holiday in England before my course begins.
- **One of the added benefits is** I'll be able to fly over in the low season, making the air ticket about half the price.

Support 2 → Mention the drawbacks（提及缺点）

- **The bad thing about this is** I may not have enough money saved up to depart earlier.
- **The main disadvantage is** I'll have less money to spend while I'm overseas.
- **One of the *weaknesses/shortcomings* is** I may not have enough time to tie up loose ends.
- **On the downside** my family will be upset that I'm leaving so suddenly.

NB

Every student in the interview will use "**if**" so be careful not to overuse it. Show how wide your range of vocabulary and grammar is by not just learning **one conditional term**.

Describing
形容

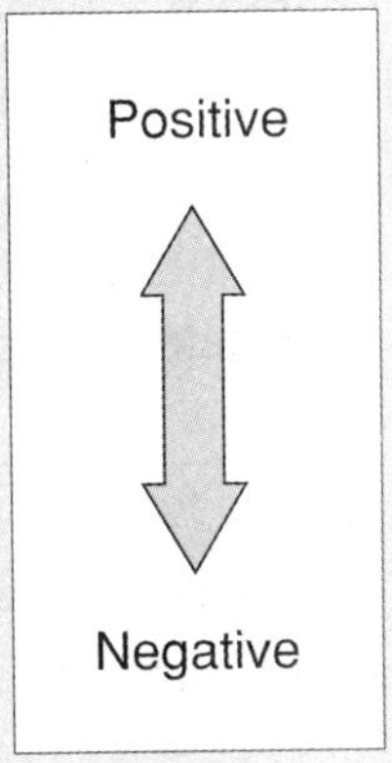

Positive or negative experience

Examiner's Questions（主考官提问）

Question → Describing （形容事物或情境）

- **What's** your hometown **like**?
- **How's** the weather in your hometown in summer?
- **What does** your best friend **look like**?
- **How do you** like your hometown?
- **Can you describe** your hometown?

Student's Answers（考生回答）

Position → State the most striking feature
（形容令人印象深刻的部分）

- My hometown's **incredibly** interesting and full of vitality.
- My town's an **absolute** hive of activity.
- My village's **one of the most** picturesque in the country.

- My city's **terribly** overcrowded.
- My place of birth's an **absolute** waste of space; nothing ever happens there.
- The small town I come from is **one of the most** backward places in the nation.

Support → Touch on personal experiences
（谈及个人经验、经历）

- **In my experience**, I have never visited a city anywhere in the world which compares with mine.
- **Speaking from experience**, as I've travelled extensively, I have never visited a city anywhere in the world which compares with mine.
- **One of my most** ***unforgettable/memorable*** **experiences was** when I visited Taipei for the first time and stayed up for 3 days straight without sleep as there were so many things to do and see.

- **If I remember rightly**, back in 1999 it won a vote on the Travel Channel for having the world's most spectacular coastline.
- **I *distinctly/vividly/vaguely* remember a time** when my parents took me hiking to a spot high in the mountains overlooking the ocean for sunrise; nothing short of spectacular!
- **I remember the time** I had growing up in my hometown **as if it were yesterday**. We were never short of something to do.
- **I will never forget the time** my relatives visited my family for Chinese New Year and there was nowhere for us to take them; everyone was bored out of their brains.
- **The time** I spent at school **is still fresh in my mind**; nothing to do after class, even less to do on weekends and absolute dead quiet holidays.

Negative experience only

- **One of my most harrowing experiences was** when I went shopping in a hypermarket and it took me 3 hours just to buy a loaf of bread and a litre of milk.
- **From bitter experience**, it wasn't until I was 13 that I saw a computer for the first time.

NB

Every student in the interview will use "**I remember**" so be careful not to overuse it. Show how wide your range of vocabulary and grammar is by not just learning one way to **talk of memories and experiences**.

Negatives
负面问题

Examiner's Questions（主考官提问）

Question → Negatives（负面问题）

- **What don't you *like/enjoy*** about your job?
- **Is there anything you don't *like/enjoy*** about your job?
- **Why don't you *like/enjoy*** your job?

Student's Answers（考生回答）

Position →State what you least *like/enjoy*
（说明你最不喜欢的事）

- **I am *sickened/disgusted* by** the work conditions.
- **I *despise/loathe/object to*** the way management handles matters.
- My colleagues are **a real turn-off** as they're always complaining and gossiping.
- **I don't think much of** my pay as it's barely enough to live off.

Support → Give a result（给出结果）

- **A direct result of** an unsatisfactory work environment **is** a decrease in productivity.
- **The implication of** unfair work conditions **is** insecure employees.
- **At the end of the day** it'll be their loss, as I'll leave the company in search of greener pastures.
- **The end result is that** they'll have a high turnover of staff, as no one will ever be happy working there.
- Incompetent staff **are the *product/result* of** substandard management skills.
- The need for side jobs ***arises/stems/comes* from** the fact that most jobs are low paying.

NB

Every student in the interview will use "**so**", so be careful not to overuse it. Show how wide your range of vocabulary and grammar is by not just learning one way to **give a result**.

Opinions
想法

Examiner's Questions（主考官提问）

Question → Opinions（想法）

- **What do you think** ***about/of*** overseas travel?
- **How do you feel about** travelling abroad?

Student's Answers（考生回答）

Position → State opinion immediately（立即表达想法）

1. **In my opinion**, travelling abroad offers the best way to gain an insight into other cultures.
2. **Personally, I feel** a holiday abroad is a great way of escaping the pressures of life in your home country.
3. **I strongly believe** taking a trip overseas is necessary, especially for kids, to learn about other cultures and nationalities.
4. **I'm of the opinion that** travel contributes a lot to globalisation.
5. **If you ask me** travelling's only beneficial if you spend enough time in a country to get to know some of the locals.
6. **To the best of my knowledge**, travelling abroad is only affordable to the wealthy and middle class.
7. **In my experience**, travelling abroad helped me become a more open-minded individual.
8. **As far as I'm concerned**, everyone should have the opportunity to visit another country so that they can reflect on their own culture.
9. **As far as I know**, travelling overseas is thought highly of in my country, but I'm not sure about other countries.
10. **To my mind** travel's adventurous and exciting, especially when you are still young.

Support → Explain a point more clearly（清楚地解释你的论点）

(The following supporting statements are numbered to correspond to the above numbered opinions.)

1. **What I'm trying to say is** the more we understand about a culture, the fewer disputes we'll have between people from different countries and the closer the world will become.
2. **That is to say**, knowing that you're unreachable by phone or email by your boss, colleagues and clients is a great load off your shoulders.
3. **In other words**, experience is the best teacher; they will learn so much more than simply absorbing the information from out of a textbook.
4. **What I mean is** people can now travel to any part of the world within 24 hours as opposed to the past when travelling could take months or even years.
5. **By this I mean**, express package tours where you visit 7 cities or countries in 7 days are a complete waste of time and money.
6. **The thing is** the poor and working class never have such an opportunity as they are struggling just to make ends meet.
7. **To put it another way**, xenophobia no longer affects me and the generalisations and stereotypes I formed as a child are now long gone.
8. **Let me *explain/rephrase* that** without travelling abroad it'll be hard to truly appreciate your own culture.
9. **All I'm saying is**, some nations embrace aspects of other cultures while others are not so welcoming.
10. **Put it this way**, there's nothing more fascinating for young people than to discover new things and places and meet new people.

NB

Every student in the interview will use "**I think**" for opinions and "**I mean**" to explain things, so be careful not to overuse them. Show how wide your range of vocabulary and grammar is by not just learning one way to **give an opinion** or **explain**.

People/ Places
人物/地点

Examiner's Questions (主考官提问)

Question → People/Places (人物 / 地点)

- **Who** is a famous person you would like to meet?
- **Which** famous **person** would you like to meet?
- **What kind of people** do you find interesting?

- **Where** would you suggest a tourist visit in your city?
- ***Which/What* place(s)** would you recommend a tourist to go to in your city?

Student's Answers (考生回答)

Position → State *who the person/where the place* is (形容该人与地方)

People

1. **There's no one like** David Beckham.
2. **Nobody compares to** Angelina Jolie.
3. **Of all people, I'd have to say** Paris Hilton.
4. **The one person who really** impresses me **is** Matt Damon.
5. **I have a soft spot for** Ewan McGregor.
6. **I think the world of** Kylie Minogue.

Places

7. **There's no place like** the National Palace Museum.
8. **Nowhere compares to** the outdoor observatory on the 89th floor of Taipei 101.
9. **Of all places, I'd have to say** the Cao Xueqin Memorial Hall.
10. **The one place which really** impresses me **is** Jiu Zhai Gou.
11. **My first choice is** the Snake Market on Hua Xi St.
12. Wu Lai with its hot springs **is as good a place as any**.

Support → Make a comparison (进行比较)

(The following supporting statements are numbered to correspond to the above numbered opinions.)

People

1. **When comparing** him **to** other soccer stars, he is so much more charismatic.

2. **If you compare** her **to** other female actors, she has so much more energy not to mention a great smile.
3. ***In/By* comparison**, other socialites are so much less daring than she is.
4. **Comparatively speaking**, his talent and determination to be successful is quite admirable.
5. **The more** I think about him, **the more** I want to ask him to marry me; not that that would ever happen apart from in my dreams.
6. She is ***getting more and more/becoming increasingly*** popular throughout the world, especially since that MTV performance she had with Justin Timberlake.

Places

7. **When comparing** it **to** other museums, its collection of Chinese artefacts is by far superior.
8. ***In/By* comparison**, other high-rise buildings and their observatory decks are simply dwarfed.
9. **If you compare** it **to** the Sun Yat Sen Memorial Hall, its grounds and Concert Halls are considerably more spacious.
10. **The more** I go there, **the more** I feel like buying and settling down in a house overlooking the river.
11. **Comparatively speaking**, it provides the most authentic oriental experience.
12. The hotels there are ***getting more and more/becoming increasingly*** opulent and up-market.

Preferences
喜好、选择

Examiner's Questions（主考官提问）

Question → Preferences（喜好、选择）

- **Do you prefer** team or individual sports?
- **Would you rather** swim at the beach or in a pool?
- **Which is better**; watching a sporting match live in a stadium or at home on TV?
- **Is** jogging **better than** swimming?
- **Is it better to** have a personal coach or train by yourself?

Student's Answers（考生回答）

Position → Make a choice（做决定）

1. **Given the choice, I'd have to say** team sports as they are so much more competitive.
2. **If I had to take a pick, I'd *favour/go for*** swimming at the beach, as you can enjoy the sunshine and gentle breeze.
3. A game at the stadium **is no match for** sitting in front of the box, as the atmosphere can really be electrifying especially when your team is winning.
4. **Give me** swimming **any day**.

Support → Add details（增加细节）

(The following supporting statements are numbered to correspond to the above numbered opinions.)

1. **Besides**, it pushes you to work harder as you don't want to let your teammates down.
2. **What's more**, it's free unlike many swimming pools.
3. **And another thing**, unlike home where you may disturb your wife or neighbours, you can shout and yell as loud as you like without upsetting the people around you.
4. It requires the use of every part of your body, **not to mention the fact that** being in the water is so much more refreshing.

- At the beach you can enjoy the open air and sunshine, make sandcastles, go body-surfing, surfing or boogie boarding, take a stroll and get a tan. **On top of all this**, it's free!
- The beach offers a wide variety of activities for families, couples and individuals. **It's also worth mentioning** that there are a number of beaches along the north and north east coast of Taiwan which are only a short car trip away from Taipei City.

Reasons
理由

Examiner's Questions（主考官提问）

Question → Reasons （有关原因、理由的问题）

- **Why** is the Internet so popular?
- **What's the reason for** the popularity of the Internet?
- **What's the cause of** the Internet's popularity?
- **How come** the Internet is so popular?

Student's Answers（考生回答）

Position → State the main reason （提出主要的原因）

More than one reason

- **One of the reasons** it's so big at the moment **is that** it offers something for everyone, from games to the latest news and even shopping.
- The sheer amount of information readily available **plays a major part in** its demand.

Only one reason

- **I'd put it down to the fact that** it's so quick, handy and useful.
- **The only reason that comes to mind is** the vast amount of knowledge that can be gained with a touch of a button.

No reason known

- **Why in the world** the Internet is so popular is **beyond me.**

Support → Contrast （对比性、相反性论调）

Subject usually stays the same

- **Then again**, it's not all it's cracked up to be as there are also many problems and dangers of the Internet.
- **All the same**, the downsides of the Internet cannot be ignored.
- **Even so**, the Internet does not always live up to expectations.
- ***Although/Even though*** the net is popular, it is so mainly with the younger generation as the elderly cannot get accustomed to all the technicalities of computer use.
- **While** the net has a lot to offer, there's nothing like talking to real people in the real world and shopping in real stores in real time.

- ***Despite/In spite of*** these obvious benefits, the dangers cannot be ignored.
- **Having said that**, the Internet does have a lot to answer for in terms of the rise in the crime rate and the amount of inappropriate and often offensive material which can be found on it.

Subject often changes

- **On the other hand**, books can still offer as much information as the Internet can.
- The Internet is good for convenient 24-hour shopping **whereas** department stores are still a much safer shopping option.
- **Alternatively**, books can also keep you well-informed.

NB

Every student in the interview will use "**but**", so be careful not to overuse it. Show how wide your range of vocabulary and grammar is by not just learning one way to **contrast information**.

Suggestions
建议

Examiner's Questions（主考官提问）

Question → Suggestions（建议）

- **What should you do** if you feel homesick when you are studying abroad?
- **What do you recommend doing** if you are homesick?
- **What do you suggest** for homesickness?

Student's Answers（考生回答）

Position → State the strongest suggestion（提出最强烈的建议）

1. **I highly recommend** making your way down to Chinatown or your local Chinese restaurant and spoiling yourself with all those favourite dishes they have.
2. **If you want my advice, you ought to** jump on to MSN and catch up with as many friends as you can from back home.
3. **No matter what, you have to** call your favourite family members back home to have a big chat about anything and everything.
4. **Take my advice**: go hang out with some other international students and tell them how you feel, in all likelihood they'll know what you're going through and give you some useful tips.
5. **You'd be well-advised to** talk to the International Student Counsellor.
6. **On no account should you** go back home.
7. **I'd strongly advise against** locking and isolating yourself in your room.

Support → Mixed strategies (for Position 5)
(综合论述)

The reason is they are the experts and deal with this kind of problem every day. **In fact**, it would be best to drop into their office when you first arrive as they conduct seminars and hold social activities to prevent you from missing home in the first place. **I distinctly remember the time** my older sister was studying abroad in New Zealand. Before we knew it, she was calling us from the international airport in Beijing asking us to pick her up. **What I'm trying to say is** get help as soon as possible, don't wait until it's too late and then end up doing something stupid.

This support includes a **reason**, **extra detail**, **personal experience** and **explanation**.

Specifying
具体提问

Examiner's Questions (主考官提问)

Question → Specifying (具体提问)

- **What** ***kind/type/sort*** **of** music do you like?
- **Which** music **style** do you like?
- **What** music **genre** do you prefer?

Student's Answers (考生回答)

Position → Indicate which one in particular (指出最特别的)

- **There are a number of** music styles I like **but I would particularly like to mention** reggae.
- **There** ***is/are*** **a wide variety of** music types I like **but I'd like to** ***single/point*** **out** R & B (Rhythm and Blues).

Support → A mix of strategies (综合论述)

The beauty of reggae is that it makes you feel like you are at the beach and that all your work pressures are left far, far away. **In comparison**, other genres add to your stress by being too noisy or getting you all hyped up. **What's more**, if you play it in the car it feels like you are going off on a road trip along the Jamaican coast to see Bob Marley. "Could You Be Loved", "Stir It Up", "Is This Love" and "Buffalo Soldier" are **just a few** great reggae hits I love to listen to. **All in all**, if you want to escape reality, there is nothing better than reggae.

This answer includes a **benefit**, **comparison**, **extra detail**, **examples** and **summary** to support the position.

Superlatives
最高级

Examiner's Questions（主考官提问）

Question → Superlatives（"最……"的提问）

- **What's the most** interesting website you know?
- **What's the best** website on the net?
- **What's your favourite** website?
- **What** website **do you** like **best**?

Student's Answers（考生回答）

Position → State what ranks the highest（最高评价的论述）

- bbc.com **takes the cake**.
- **The pick of the bunch would have to be** bbc.com.
- **Nothing compares to** bbc.com.
- bbc.com **is head and shoulders above the rest**.
- **You can't beat** bbc.com **for** sheer content and in the cyber industry they say "content is king".
- bbc.com **runs rings around the others**.
- bbc.com **is streets ahead of the rest**.
- bbc.com **puts the rest to shame**.

Support → Mixed strategies（综合论述）

What makes it a cut above other news websites **is the fact that** it has something for everyone. It has online radio stations, about 40 actually, the latest news, educational sections and shopping **to mention but a few** of the services it offers. **A direct result of** having such a thorough and detailed site is people will use it as a one-stop shop for all their internet needs. **Then again**, I must admit CNN.com does a pretty good job too.

This support includes a **reason**, **examples**, **result** and **contrast**.

Time
时间

Examiner's Questions（主考官提问）

Question → Time（关于时间的提问）

- **How often** do you go to the library?
- **How many times** have you been to the library this year?
- **When** do you prefer to read?
- **What time** of day do you prefer to read?
- **How much time** do you spend reading every week?
- **How long** have you been learning English?

Student's Answers（考生回答）

Position → State the frequency, time or duration（陈述频率、时间或持续性）

Frequency

- **I've never been known to** visit the library.
- I go to the library **once in a blue moon**.
- I make it to the library ***on and off/now and again/every so often/from time to time/every once in a while/whenever I get the chance***.
- I've been to the library **hundreds of times**.

Time

- **There's no such time as** bedtime.
- **Of all the times, I'd have to say** just before I go to sleep.
- **The one time I really** enjoy reading **is** on lazy Sunday afternoons.

Duration

- **I spend a greater part of** every weekend reading.
- I've been learning English **longer than you can imagine**.
- **I've spent** ***days/weeks/months/years/a lifetime*** learning English.

Support → Mixed strategies（综合论述）

The chief reason why I avoid libraries **is** they lack efficiency and convenience especially since the advent of the Internet.

Put it this way, who can be bothered travelling all the way to the local library, sifting through catalogues and walking aimlessly through aisles and aisles of bookshelves when at the touch of a button a search engine can do all the looking for you from the comfort of your own home? **Another weakness of** libraries is that you may need to wait for days for the book you want if someone has beaten you to it. **At the end of the day**, it's all about increasing your pace of life; when we want something, we want it now.

This support includes a **reason**, **explanation**, **drawback** and **result**.

Yes/No
是与非的提问

Examiner's Questions（主考官提问）

Question → Yes/No（是与非的提问）

1. **Are you** good at dancing?
2. **Do you** think watching TV is better than reading a book?
3. **Will you** celebrate if you pass the IELTS exam?
4. **Have you** been living in your current house long?
5. **Are there** any interesting places to visit in your hometown?
6. **Did you** like high school?

Student's Answers（考生回答）

Position → Say yes or no but in an alternative way（用不同的方式来表示 yes 或 no）

- For "**yes**": definitely, for sure, without a doubt, naturally, of course, indeed, certainly, I'm afraid so
- For "**no**": not at all, no way, I'm afraid not, certainly not, not really, of course not, you must be kidding

NB

All yes/no positions need to be coupled with one of the previous positions to be complete. For instance no. 1 is also an ability question, no. 2 opinion, no. 3 conditional, no. 4 time duration, no. 5 place and no. 6 identifying.

Support → Mixed strategies（综合论述）

You must be kidding! **I can't** dance **to save my life.** **One of my most harrowing experiences** was the school formal when everyone took a turn in the spotlight dancing with their partner. I **not only** made a fool of myself **but also** embarrassed my partner when I accidentally pushed her over and we ended up in a rather compromising position. **Generally speaking**, you will never see me on a dance floor again, not in this lifetime anyway.

This support includes a "**no**" response, **proficiency level**, **personal experience**, **extra detail** and **summary**.

Speaking Test Part 2

In this section of the test you will be given a topic card and asked to speak on the topic for 1 to 2 minutes. Before you talk you have one minute to think about what you are going to say and you may make some notes during this time.

This section will detail the best ways of making notes, how to give introductions that leave a positive impression and how to develop your ideas.

在口语测试的 Part 2 中，考生需要针对“话题卡”的问题发表 1～2 分钟的意见。拿到话题卡后，考生会有 1 分钟的准备时间。本章将会详述该如何很好地利用这 1 分钟，并教你如何有效地做笔记及阐述你的意见。

Making Notes 记笔记

Do not waste your precious one minute preparation time as you will not get any extra points for starting your speech early. Use the time given to make as many notes as you can so you don't run out of ideas to talk about. Moreover, so you can fluently complete the 2 minutes that you should be talking for. During this one minute you will also have the opportunity to organise your ideas so you can talk about them coherently and in a logical order which will cause less strain on the examiner.

When you make notes, only write down the key points and not every detail of your speech in full sentences. So what are key points? Key points are ideas in 1 or 2 words so that when you look at them, you immediately know what to say and how to keep talking.

Remember it's difficult talking for 2 minutes so making the right notes is essential for success in Part 2. Even though the topic card will give you 4 points to help you with ideas on how to develop your conversation, this is often not enough for most people, so making more notes will ensure you can keep speaking for 2 minutes.

Too often students make notes that do not assist them much at all. The following will teach you how to make the best notes for the 5 most common topics in Part 2: people, places, things/objects, activities, time/events.

别浪费 1 分钟的准备时间，早点开始回答问题并不会加分。利用这 1 分钟，尽可能写下最多的笔记，以免发表意见的时间不足 2 分钟；另外，组织好你的意见，避免散乱没组织的回答。做笔记时无需写下整个段落，只要写下能提示的关键字即可。

做好笔记是 Part 2 得高分的一大关键，为确保能持续发表 2 分钟的意见，依赖话题卡的 4 点提示是不够的。充分利用时间，整理出充足的意见才是重点。

本章以 IELTS 口试最常出现的 5 个主题——人物、地点、物品、活动、时间 / 事件为例，提供有效做好笔记的方法。

Student's notes on the topic "Describe a famous person":

学生的笔记——形容一位名人

1. Jackie Chan
2. Big nose
3. Strong
4. Good body
5. A little short
6. Rush hour
7. Shanghai Noon
8. Hong Kong Kung Fu movies
9. About *50/60* years old
10. Married
11. 2 kids I think

- Are these good notes?

  NO!
- Why not?

  Many points could be grouped together but aren't. The order is illogical.

Better notes may look like this:

较好的笔记

1. Jackie Chan
2. Background information
3. Appearance
4. Movies

■ Are these better notes?

YES!

■ Why?

Points 2 to 5 of the student's notes are grouped together under appearance. Points 6 to 8 are grouped under movies. Points 9 to 11 are grouped under background information.

The right notes look like this:

正确的笔记

1. (Name)
2. Background information
3. Appearance
4. Personality
5. *Jobs/Studies*
6. Lifestyle
7. Accomplishments
8. What I *like/dislike*
9. Influence

■ Are these the right notes?

YES!

■ Why?

The notes are very general and different from each other (if they are too similar or specific it will be difficult to expand upon). These notes can be used to describe any person not just Jackie Chan so you only have to remember one set of notes for each type of Part 2 topic.

Useful Notes
实用笔记

Below are notes you can generally use for most topics. However you may need to pick and choose.
以下的笔记适用于大部分的主题。

Describing places

1. location
2. scenery
3. attractions
4. industry
5. amenities
6. people
7. food
8. history
9. *good/bad* points

Describing people

1. name
2. background information
3. appearance
4. personality
5. *jobs/studies*
6. lifestyle
7. accomplishments
8. influence
9. what I *like/dislike*

Describing objects

1. background
2. appearance
3. functions
4. differences between similar objects
5. *good/bad* points

Describing *time/events*

1. time
2. place
3. significance

4. background
5. people
6. activities

Describing activities

1. where
2. when
3. who
4. how
5. equipment
6. *good/bad* points

Introductory Statements
开头句

The following sentences are ways of starting your Part 2 talk. They are very general statements and can be used for a variety of topics. Be aware however that they cannot be used for absolutely every topic. The following topic card will be used to show you how they can be used.

以下列出的"开头句"可以应用在 Part 2 的测试中。它们适用于大部分的主题。以下面的题目为例：

> Describe a TV programme you find informative.
> You should say:
> ■ what it is
> ■ what content it has
> ■ how often you can watch it
> and explain why you like it.

1. There are a number of (topic) but the one I'd particularly like to mention today is (your answer).
   There are a number of TV programmes I find informative but the one I'd particularly like to mention today is "Super Structures" on *Discovery*.

2. When talking about (topic), it's worth pointing out (your answer).
   When talking about TV programmes I find informative, it's worth pointing out "Super Structures" on *Discovery*.

3. In regards to (topic), (your answer) *rates/deserves* a mention.

   In regards to TV programmes I find informative, "Super Structures" on *Discovery* rates a mention.

4. If I have to say a few words on (topic), I'd like to bring up (your answer).

   If I have to say a few words on TV programmes I find informative, I'd like to bring up "Super Structures" on *Discovery*.

5. There is one (topic) that I always enjoy talking about and that is (your answer).

   There is one TV programme that I always enjoy talking about and that is "Super Structures" on *Discovery*.

6. To tell you the truth I don't have much to say on (topic) but I'll do my best to talk about (your answer).

   To tell you the truth I don't have much to say on TV programmes but I'll do my best to talk about "Super Structures" on *Discovery*.

NB

Point 6 can be used when little is known about the topic.

Sample Topics and Sample Answers
各类型问题及回答范例

People
人物

Sample topics are listed below followed by a sample answer. Pay particular attention to how each note is expanded on so as to fulfill the 2-minute limit.

下面提供各类型主题的常见问题集。每个主题附上 1 个回答范例。特别注意回答范例的组织架构，学习如何扩展回答内容以达到 2 分钟的时限。

Sample Topics

Describe **a young child that you know**.
You should say:
- who the person is
- how you know him/her
- what he/she is like

and explain why you like him/her.

Describe **an old person that you know**.
You should say:
- who the person is
- how you know him/her
- what he/she is like

and explain why you like him/her.

Describe **a person that has influenced you**.
You should say:
- who the person is
- how you know him/her
- what he/she is like

and explain why you like him/her.

Describe **a teacher that you like.**
You should say:
- who the person is
- what he/she taught you
- what he/she is like

and explain why you like him/her.

Describe **a famous person from your country**.
You should say:
- who the person is
- what he/she is famous for
- what he/she is like

and explain why you like him/her.

Describe **your best friend.**
You should say:
- who the person is
- how you know him/her
- what he/she is like

and explain why you like him/her.

Describe **an artist from your country**.
You should say:
- who the person is
- why he/she is famous
- what his/her works are like

and explain why you like him/her.

Describe **your ideal husband/wife**.
You should say:
- what qualities he/she should have
- what he/she looks like
- what you would do together

and explain why you would like him/her.

Describe **a typical person from your country**.
You should say:
- what qualities he/she has
- what he/she looks like
- what he/she does

and explain what you like about him/her.

Describe **your favourite family member**.
You should say:
- who the person is
- how close your relationship is
- what he/she is like

and explain why you like him/her.

Sample Answer (People)

Describe **an artist from your country**.
You should say:
- who the person is
- why he/she is famous
- what his/her works are like

and explain why you like him/her.

Support and Development

Intro

To tell you the truth, I don't know much about artists in general, let alone those from my own country, but I'll do my best to talk about "Ken Done" who's somewhat of a celebrity in Australia.

Background information

Now, I believe he resides in Sydney though I'm not entirely sure. The reason why I think he's from Sydney is possibly due to the fact that he always draws the Sydney city scenery—such things as the Harbour Bridge and Opera House.

Appearance

He's a man who's probably at least in his 40s as he has greying hair as far as I can recall. The only other feature of his appearance that comes to mind is his signature moustache that he never seems to shave off.

Character

In terms of personality, my guess, if his artwork's a valid indication, is that he's a very vibrant and positive person. His artwork's often filled with bright colours and has a very carefree feel to it.

Accomplishments

His artwork is mostly commonly found in airports and duty free shops as he seems to be a hit with tourists. Therefore his art is not just sold as paintings but can also be bought on T-shirts, cups, towels or even hats. Anything a tourist would want as a souvenir, his artwork can be found on. Although I still come across his pieces every now and again, I'd say the peak of his career was probably in the 80s and to some extent the 90s.

Lifestyle

In regards to his lifestyle, apart from painting obviously, he can be seen on TV programmes every so often and charity events. He also seems like quite a family man to me though I'm not sure if he's married or not or even if he has any kids.

What you *like/dislike*

What I like about him is the fact that even though he probably is not the best painter in the world he can become rich and successful with just a simple idea. What I'm saying is that he's not the most skilled and talented but he's quite clever and creative.

Influence

This has inspired me in a couple of ways. Firstly that keeping things simple is important; making things too complex is not necessarily a sign of intelligence. And secondly, a small idea can go a long way if you believe in it and work hard at it.

NB

If you just follow the suggestions on the topic card it will probably not be enough for most people to keep talking for 1-2 minutes so make sure you make lots of extra notes so you are never short of something to say. You don't need to mention every point on the topic card as they are there as suggestions to help you to extend your answer and keep talking. You must however stick to the topic—that may not change.

Places
地点

Sample Topics

Describe **your favourite city**.
You should say:
- where the place is
- what you can do there
- what makes it different from other cities

and explain why you like it.

Describe **a country you would love to visit**.
You should say:
- where the place is
- what you can do there
- what makes it special

and explain why you like it.

Describe **the most boring place you have been to**.
You should say:
- where the place is
- what you can do there
- what makes it so boring

and explain why you dislike it.

Describe **a place of historical significance in your country**.
You should say:
- where the place is
- what you can do there
- how old it is

and explain why it is a significant part of your culture.

Describe **the house you live in**.
You should say:
- where your house is
- what it looks like on the outside
- what features it has inside

and explain what you like about it.

Describe **a popular tourist attraction in your country**.
You should say:
- where it is
- what you can do there
- what makes it so popular

and explain what you like about it.

Describe **a place that is or should be heritage listed by your government**.
You should say:
- where the place is
- what you can do there
- what it is threatened by

and explain why it should be protected.

Describe **a place you frequent with friends**.
You should say:
- where the place is
- what you can do there
- how popular it is

and explain why you like it.

Sample Answer (Places)

Describe your **favourite shopping centre**.
You should say:
- where it is
- what you can do there
- what makes it special

and explain why you like it.

Support and Development

Intro

When talking about shopping centres, I believe the Miramar shopping complex deserves a mention.

Location

The mall's in Da Zhi which is just near my house actually, only about a 5-10 minute walk. For most people though it's not the most handy of locations as the MRT line will not be opened for another 2 years and there are not so many bus routes travelling out that way either. What this means is if you wanna go, you basically need to have a car or motorbike. Fortunately though they offer free underground parking which has kept people going back there I think.

Attractions

The main attraction would have to be the Ferris Wheel which I heard is actually the second biggest in Asia. The first being in Japan I believe. This has made the centre popular not just for families with young kids but also for young couples in search of a little romance. There's one other attraction—that of the IMAX theatre. I've actually only been to it once but it was quite an enjoyable 3-D experience of dinosaurs.

Amenities and facilities

Apart from that, all the other services they offer are the same as other major shopping centres like Sogo, Mitsukoshi, and Takashimaya. Some of the stores I frequent would be their food court, the Eslite Bookstore, TGI Friday's and the ice cream shop but I forget what it was called, not Häagen Dazs anyway, the other one.

People

The people that go there, as I said before, are mainly families with young children and young couples but if they have an event on there, which they often do, it could attract all sorts of people. I distinctly remember once when I was there and it was just packed with baseball fans as one of the local teams was there to pose for photos with bystanders.

Background/ history

There's not too much to say about the background or history of the centre. All I seem to know is that it was opened back in 2004 if I remember rightly as that was the same year I moved into the area myself. That's how I remember.

Conclusion

All in all, I often have my most memorable shopping experiences there.

NB

If you just follow the suggestions on the topic card it will probably not be enough for most people to keep talking for 1-2 minutes so make sure you make lots of extra notes so you are never short of something to say. You don't need to mention every point on the topic card as they are there as suggestions to help you to extend your answer and keep talking. You must however stick to the topic—that may not change.

Things/ Objects
物品

Sample Topics

Describe **the most expensive thing you own.**
You should say:
- what it is
- what it looks like
- what functions it has

and explain why you like it.

Describe **something useful that you own.**
You should say:
- what it is
- what it looks like
- what functions it has

and explain why it is useful.

Describe **a car that you would like to own.**
You should say:
- what it is
- what it looks like
- what functions it has

and explain why you like it.

Describe **something you cannot live without.**
You should say:
- what it is
- what it looks like
- what functions it has

and explain why you can't live without it.

Describe **a toy you played with as a child.**
You should say:
- what it was
- what it looked like
- what functions it had

and explain why you liked it.

Describe **the clothes you like to wear.**
You should say:
- the style of the clothes
- the quality of the clothes
- the cost of the clothes

and explain why you like it.

Describe **an electronic device you can use well.**
You should say:
- what it is
- what it looks like
- what functions it has

and explain why you like it.

Describe **a product that is made in your country.**
You should say:
- what it is
- what it looks like
- what functions it has

and explain how popular it is.

Describe **a great invention**.
You should say:
- what it is
- what it looks like
- what functions it has

and explain why it is so great.

Describe **something that you have lost**.
You should say:
- what it was
- how you lost it
- how extensively you looked for it

and explain how important it was.

Describe **something you are scared of**.
You should say:
- what it is
- how long you have been scared of it
- why it is so scary

and explain how you could overcome the fear.

Sample Answer (Things/Objects)

Describe **a toy you played with as a child**.
You should say:
- what it was
- what it looked like
- what functions it had

and explain why you liked it.

Support and Development

Intro

Just like all kids, there were quite a number of toys that I'd play with but the one I'd particularly like to talk about today is my toy car racing track.

Background

As far as I can recall, I got it from my parents as a Christmas present back when I was still in primary school aged around 8 or 9, I think. It was a big deal to get a car racing track back then as these electronically powered toys had not been around so long; no more having to use your hands to push the car along was a big thing!

Appearance

If memory serves me right, there were lots of possible configurations for the track but I only ever worked out one of them which was the figure of 8. That was enough though to keep me occupied for hours on end. It came with the lot, everything from stadiums to bridges. In fact, it included a whole range of stickers too which you had to stick all over the track and cars.

Functions

How it worked was actually not so complex—I'm sure the racing tracks on the market these days are far more sophisticated. It basically came with 2 cars and 2 things which were like remote controls. You'd place the car on the track and then push a lever down on the so-called remote control which would act as the accelerator. There were no brakes just the gas! The lighter you pushed down though, the slower it would go. In terms of functions though, it didn't really offer much.

Comparisons with similar objects

At that time, I think there were better models out on the market. As I recall, some had a loop while others had tracks climbing a wall. My track was actually quite modest in comparison but as a kid you don't know any better and it was still one of my most memorable toys.

Good/bad points

The best thing about it was having races with friends or my Dad and what made it so exciting was one section of the track which would narrow to only allow one car through—that was the time the spectacular crashes would happen.

Conclusion

Eventually, as I got older I progressed onto bigger remote controlled cars but that's a different story. The first always stays in your mind fresher.

NB

If you just follow the suggestions on the topic card it will probably not be enough for most people to keep talking for 1-2 minutes so make sure you make lots of extra notes so you are never short of something to say. You don't need to mention every point on the topic card as they are there as suggestions to help you to extend your answer and keep talking. You must however stick to the topic—that may not change.

Activities

活动

Sample Topics

Describe **a dangerous sport.**
You should say:
■ what it is
■ what equipment is needed
■ how to play it
and explain what makes it so dangerous.

Describe **a relaxing activity.**
You should say:
■ what it is
■ where it is enjoyed
■ what is needed
and explain what makes it so relaxing.

Describe **a typical day at *work/school.***
You should say:
■ what you do
■ who you interact with
■ what you *like/dislike*
and explain what is most difficult.

Describe **a game you played as a child.**
You should say:
■ what it was
■ what equipment was needed
■ how to play it
and explain what made it so enjoyable.

Describe **your computer habits**.
You should say:
■ what you use it for
■ how often you use it
■ when you use it
and explain what you would do without it.

Describe **something you are learning now**.
You should say:
■ what it is
■ how you learn it
■ why you are learning it
and explain what is most difficult about it.

Describe **a way to stay healthy**.
You should say:
■ what it is
■ what is needed
■ how popular it is
and explain why it is beneficial.

Describe **an activity you do with your family**.
You should say:
■ what it is
■ what you *like/dislike* about it
■ how often you do it
and explain why you do it.

Sample Answer (Activities)

Describe **an outdoor activity you enjoy**.
You should say:
- what it is
- what equipment is needed
- who takes part

and explain what makes it so enjoyable.

Support and Development

Intro

There's one activity that I always enjoy doing and talking about and that is fishing for prawns.

Where

There are many places you can go to for this which are usually on the outskirts of Taipei, but one of the most famous spots would have to be Wai Shuang Xi where the main street is just lined with pool after pool of prawns. These pools are nestled in the mountains making it quite a natural experience despite the fact that prawns are already conveniently place in pools for you.

When

Most people head to these places on weekends but I prefer to go on a weekday when there aren't so many people competing for a catch. Most astonishingly of all though is the fact that most of these places are open 24 hours.

Who

I often go with friends as it's a good way of relaxing. Apart from dropping in your line, you can also have a beer and good old chat with your mates. Many families with young kids also make their way there as kids enjoy the thrill of catching a prawn.

How & equipment

It's quite a simple activity that anyone could do as everything is prepared for you. When you arrive they give you the rods and bait. All you have to do is unwind your line, put on some bait and then cast it. There's a small buoy on the line and when that submerges it means you have a prawn. Pull your line up, take the little fellow off and place it in a net for later. However you may see some guys who have turned it into a fine art. They have their own rods and measure the depth of water and length of line to ensure they catch the maximum number of prawns.

Good/bad points

For me though it's all about fun. Everyone's pretty much guaranteed of a catch and you can even make it into a little competition with your mates or family members to see who catches the most in the allocated time. An added benefit is the fact that you can eat your catch too, meaning you have entertainment plus dinner. On the downside, it actually ends up being much cheaper to buy the prawns at the shop than catching them yourself.

NB

If you just follow the suggestions on the topic card it will probably not be enough for most people to keep talking for 1-2 minutes so make sure you make lots of extra notes so you are never short of something to say. You don't need to mention every point on the topic card as they are there as suggestions to help you to extend your answer and keep talking. You must however stick to the topic—that may not change.

Time/Events
时间/事件

Sample Topics

Describe **a natural disaster that occurred in your country**.
You should say:
- what happened
- what effect it had on your country
- what was done about it

and explain what made it so devastating.

Describe **a memorable trip you have had**.
You should say:
- where you went
- what you did
- who you went with

and explain what made it so memorable.

Describe **a festival from your country**.
You should say:
- what happens
- what customs there are
- who is involved

and explain what significance it has.

Describe **an exciting competition you *watched/took part in***.
You should say:
- when it was
- what happened
- who was involved

and explain what made it so exciting.

Describe **what the future may be like.**
You should say:
- what the people may be like
- what the environment be like
- how different it will be

and explain whether it will be better or worse.

Describe **a stressful moment in your life.**
You should say:
- when it was
- what caused the stress
- what the stress led to

and explain how you overcame the stressful situation.

Describe **the worst weather you have experienced.**
You should say:
- when it was
- what the weather was like
- what damage it caused

and explain what made is so terrible.

Describe **a party you have been to.**
You should say:
- when it was
- what kind of party it was
- who went

and explain what you liked about it.

Sample Answer (Time/Events)

Describe **a wedding from your country**.
You should say:
- what happens
- what customs there are
- how many people are involved

and explain what makes it special.

Support and Development

Intro

To be honest, I don't have much experience with weddings but I think I've seen enough movies to be able to discuss what a western wedding is like.

Time

Weddings as I'm sure you know can happen at any age—even the elderly get married these days. The time of celebration can also vary, though one of the most popular times would probably be sunset especially if you're having an outdoor ceremony. Receptions can also be at lunchtime but more often than not are in the evening.

Place

Outdoor ceremonies are all the rage these days with churches now only for more conservative or possibly more exclusive weddings. The reception will usually be taken indoors to say a restaurant or hotel. Budgets do range between couples and so do venues accordingly.

Customs

The only custom that comes to mind is the bride must wear something borrowed, something blue, something old and something new. I'm not sure how many people do this. Many consider the best customs to be before the wedding. The bucks and hens nights are classic examples.

People

Wedding sizes can vary considerably. While some opt for small private weddings with just family and close friends, others opt for more lavish and extravagant weddings where pretty much everyone they've ever known in their lives is invited.

Activities

There are a number of activities throughout the day, not necessarily in this order, but including such things as speeches, throwing confetti over the bride and groom as they leave the altar, cutting of the cake, dancing and throwing a bouquet over the bride's shoulder to indicate who'll be the next to get hitched. Oh, and of course, everyone prepares a gift for the newlyweds which is placed on a table at the reception.

Significance

These days, especially by the younger generation, the significance of marriage often comes under attack. This is possibly due to the fact that we're so much more accepting of de facto relationships. It's also questioned because of the over 50% divorce rate that most western societies have been experiencing for quite some time now.

Conclusion

What makes it special though is it's a great opportunity for all the family and friends to come together for a truly happy occasion. Everybody loves to see newlyweds as it gives you the chance to reflect on those around you who you really love.

NB

If you just follow the suggestions on the topic card it will probably not be enough for most people to keep talking for 1-2 minutes so make sure you make lots of extra notes so you are never short of something to say. You don't need to mention every point on the topic card as they are there as suggestions to help you to extend your answer and keep talking. You must however stick to the topic—that may not change.

Speaking Test Part 3

QPS Strategy
QPS 应考策略

Identify the **Question**

State a **Position**

Offer **Support**

In Part 3 of the IELTS you will have 4-5 minutes to respond to questions related to the Part 2 topic. These questions will often be somewhat unfamiliar to you and may seem quite academic. This is the most difficult part of the test but remember your English is assessed not by your intelligence so producing an answer should be your first concern.

Part 3 的时间约 4～5 分钟，是口试最难的部分。这部分的问题主要是由 Part 2 的话题卡延伸而来，多半是你不太熟悉的领域，而且较为学术性。但记住，口试是在考查你的英语能力而非智力。

This section follows the QPS strategy, so after identifying the question, promptly provide a position and then continue on to support that position. Make sure everything you say relates to your position or you may confuse the examiner. However, unlike Part 2, there is no preparation time in Part 3.

有效应用QPS 应考策略(问题—定位—支持)，针对主考官提出的问题，精准定位，提出佐证，尽可能地发表意见才是得分关键!

Types of Questions and How to Answer Them
各类型问题及答题方式

Predicting
预测

Examiner's Questions（主考官提问）

Question → Predicting （预测）

- **How will** crime ***change/develop*** **in the next few decades?**
- **Do you think** crime **will be different in 50 years time?**
- **Could you** ***speculate/predict*** **what** crime **will be like 10 years from now?**

Student's Answers（考生回答）

Position → State certainty （确定性的陈述）

Probably

- **In all probability**, there'll be an increase in internet-based crimes.
- **There's every possibility** that internet crimes will be on the increase.
- **It's more than likely** that the internet crime rate will increase significantly.

Probably not

- **There's** ***little/no*** **chance of** the crime rate ever decreasing.
- **There's a** ***remote/slight*** **prospect of** the crime rate decreasing.

NB

Every student in the interview will use "**maybe**" so be careful not to overuse it. Show how wide your range of vocabulary and grammar is by not just learning one way to **express possibility**.

Support → Mixed strategies （综合论述）

I'd attribute it to the fact that criminals find it easier to hide their identity and remain undetected as they prey on innocent web surfers. **For instance**, the computer savvy can steal any of your personal data from your birth date to your credit card number without your knowledge as technology these days can track every move you make on the net. **While** it's never happened to me, I've heard of a number of people who have had the **bitter experience** of things showing up on their credit card bill that they didn't actually buy. **As a result of** continued technological improvements, crime will also keep developing.

This support contains a **reason**, **example**, **contrast**, **experience** and **result**.

Past Development
过去的发展

Examiner's Questions（主考官提问）

Question → Past development （过去的发展）

- **How was** education **different 50 years ago**?
- **Do you think** education **has changed much since your parents were young**?
- **Could you evaluate how** education **has developed over the past few decades**?

Student's Answers（考生回答）

Position → State how *different/similar* it was
（指出不同处 / 相似处）

Completely different

- **It's a whole new ball game these days.**
- The education system **nowadays bears no relation to the past.**
- The education system **these days is worlds apart from the past.**

Very different

- **It was a radically different world** when my parents were young.
- **It was *considerably/significantly/refreshingly/strikingly* different** 50 years ago.
- **Today's** education system **is a far cry from the past**.

A little different

- **It was *slightly/subtly* different** a few decades ago.

Support → Mixed strategies （综合论述）

A prime example is technology which in the past was unheard of; these days we have computers, e-learning, teaching through PowerPoint presentations, dictionaries on CD-ROM, and past lessons recorded on mp3. **In stark contrast**, my parents only had paper, pen and chalkboards. **A direct result of** this kind of technology is an overall improvement in education standards. **It's also worth mentioning** that nowadays there is no more corporal punishment allowed in the classroom.

This support includes an **example**, **contrast**, **result** and **extra detail**.

Causes of Problems
问题的原因

Examiner's Questions（主考官提问）

Question → Causes of problems （问题的原因）

- **Why do you think** there is an increase in private car use?
- **What is the cause of** traffic congestion?
- **What is the reason for** having your own car?
- **Could you explain why** people want to have their own car?
- **What explanations could you provide for** the increase in private car ownership?
- **Could you justify** the need for your own private car?

Student's Answers（考生回答）

Position → State reason （说明原因）

More than one reason

- **One of the reasons** most people own a car **is** that the public transportation system in most cities is inadequate and inefficient.
- The inadequate and inefficient public transportation system **plays a part in** people wanting their own car.

Only one reason

- **The only reason that comes to mind is** convenience.
- **The root of the problem is** everyone's hunger for a higher standard of living and disrespect for the environment.
- **I'd put it down to** convenience.

No reason known

- **Why in the world** people still insist on driving their own car is beyond me.

Support → Mixed strategies （综合论述）

I'd put it before the transportation officials to radically improve the public transportation system by increasing the number of routes and lines of all forms of travel. Convenience will arise **as a result** and that is what everyone is looking for. **On the downside**, it means that in all probability there'll be a hike in taxes which is something that nobody wants. **All in all**, authorities are caught between a rock and a hard place in this matter.

This support includes a **suggestion**, **result**, **drawback** and **summary**.

Results
结果

Examiner's Questions（主考官提问）

Question → Results （结果）

- **What are the effects of** unemployment?
- **How does** unemployment **affect** society?
- **What effect does** unemployment **have on** society?
- **What does** unemployment **lead to**?
- **What does** unemployment **result in**?

Student's Answers（考生回答）

Position → State result （表明结果、决定）

- **There are a number of *outcomes/results/consequences/after-effects/implications*, the main one being** a weaker economy.
- **The main impact of** unemployment **is** a weaker economy.
- **It has a far-reaching effect on** the economy.

Support → Mixed strategies （综合论述）

It stands to reason that the more unemployed people there are, the less productive a nation will be. **What's more,** there is extra pressure on taxpayers to foot the welfare bills that the government has to fork out for such people. **Then again** if the government refuses to support the jobless, then it may encourage them to look more vigilantly for a job and be less reliant on welfare support. **All I'm saying is** those out of work need to be strongly advised to find a job ASAP for the good of society.

This support includes a **reason**, **extra detail**, **contrast** and **explanation**.

Solutions/ Suggestions
解决方案/建议

Examiner's Questions（主考官提问）

Question → Solutions/Suggestions（解决方案 / 建议）

- **How could the problem of** the ageing population **be solved**?
- **What can be done about** the potential ageing population crisis?
- **What could the** ***government/authorities*** **do to improve** conditions for the elderly?
- **Could you suggest some ways to make** society **better** for the elderly?

Student's Answers（考生回答）

Position → State the strongest suggestion（提出最强烈的建议）

Should do

- **I'd put it before the authorities to** take swift measures that encourage more young people to become physicians and nurses before it's too late.
- **They may as well** start constructing more hospitals now.
- **I highly recommend** they improve the medical facilities.
- **If you want my advice, they ought to** allocate more resources to medical research.
- **No matter what, they have to** take swift action before it's too late.
- Health officials **would be well-advised to** start streamlining all medical procedures and administration.

Shouldn't do

- **On no account should they remain idle**.
- **I'd strongly advise against** sweeping the problem under the rug.

Support → Mixed strategies（综合论述）

The fact that the elderly will outnumber the workforce in the not so distant future will **give rise to** a number of issues **such as** a strain on medical resources and welfare benefits. **By this I mean**, more doctors, nurses, pharmacists and old age carers will be needed, **yet** the workforce will not be large enough **due to** a drop in the birth rate. **Secondly**, taxpayers will also have a heavy burden as they'll be expected to support pensioners **in terms of** medical bills, accommodation and general living expenses. **On the whole**, it'll be a tall order for society to overcome this future obstacle.

This support includes a **result**, **examples**, **explanation**, **contrast**, **reason**, **extra detail**, another **reason**, more **examples** and **summary**.

Advantages/ Disadvantages
优点 / 缺点

Examiner's Questions（主考官提问）

Question → Advantages/Disadvantages（优点 / 缺点）

- **What are the advantages and disadvantages of** shopping online?
- **What are the benefits and drawbacks of** shopping online?
- **What are the pros and cons of** shopping online?
- **What are the merits and shortcomings of** shopping online?
- **What are the strengths and weaknesses of** shopping online?
- **What are the arguments for and against** shopping online?
- **What are the positive and negative sides of** shopping online?
- **What are the pluses and minuses of** shopping online?

Student's Answers（考生回答）

Position 1 → State the advantages in an alternative way（说明优点）

- **The *advantages/benefits/pros/merits/strengths/positive sides/pluses* are** it provides a greater variety of shops, you don't need to walk around or pay for parking and it's open 24 hours all year round.
- **The beauty of** online shopping **is** it provides a greater variety of shops, you don't need to walk around or pay for parking and it's open 24 hours all year round.
- **What makes** online shopping **so good is** it provides a greater variety of shops, you don't need to walk around or pay for parking and it's open 24 hours all year round.

Support 1 → Mixed strategies（综合论述）

Put it this way, one minute you could be shopping for Prada products in Italy and with the simple click of a button be in Japan shopping for a PDA. **Above all** you don't have to pay for any plane tickets, taxi fares or take up any time travelling from one shop to the next.

This support includes an **explanation** and **extra detail**.

NB

If the examiner asks you to state the advantages and disadvantages you must mention both—you may be penalised if you don't. So add the position and support below to any advantages/disadvantages question.

Position 2 → State the disadvantages in an alternative way（说明缺点）

- **On the downside** it's unsafe to give out credit card details on the net, you can't try on any clothes you may like and you have to wait for delivery.
- **Having said that, the *disadvantages/drawbacks/cons/shortcomings/weaknesses/negative sides/minuses* are** it's unsafe to give out credit card details on the net, you can't try on any clothes you may like and you have to wait for delivery.

Support 2 → Mixed strategies（综合论述）

What this means is, the Internet can also be seen as inconvenient. **That is to say,** there are so many more things to worry you **like** "Did they receive payment? Will they honour it? Will they send it to the right address? Will the clothes fit? What happens if they send the wrong item?" **In a nutshell**, all these things cannot be guaranteed before purchase.

This support includes 2 **explanations**, **examples** and a **summary.**

Comparing
比较

Examiner's Questions（主考官提问）

Question → Comparing（比较）

- **Could you compare the similarities and differences between** modern **and** traditional architecture?
- **Could you assess how** modern **and** traditional architecture **is *different/similar*?**
- **Could you examine the main differences between** modern **and** traditional architecture?

Student's Answers（考生回答）

Position → State similarities *and/or* differences
（陈述相似性 / 相异处）

Different

- **One of the major contrasts is** the design.
- **What sets** modern architecture **apart is** the design.
- **Unlike** traditional architecture, the design of modern homes is more aesthetically pleasing.

Same

- **The most striking resemblance is** they still serve the same purpose.
- **One of the similarities includes** them both serving the same purpose.
- **They are *identical/alike* in terms of** the purpose they serve.

Support 1 → Mixed strategies (for expressing differences)
（综合论述）

Classic examples include the rooms. Kitchens these days are smaller **due to the fact that** we eat out more often; living rooms are more spacious **so that** we can enjoy our relaxation time more and bathrooms are more luxurious **as a result of** being obsessed with hygiene and cleanliness.

Support 2 → Mixed Strategies (for expressing similarities)
(综合论述)

When comparing homes of the past to those of the present, they both have a kitchen for preparing food, bedrooms for sleeping, bathrooms for personal hygiene and living rooms for rest and relaxation. **All in all**, nothing much has changed **as** shelter is a basic need of mankind.

These supporting statements include **examples**, **reasons**, **purpose**, **result**, **comparison** and **summary**.

Agree/Disagree
同意/不同意

Examiner's Questions（主考官提问）

Question → Agree/Disagree（同意 / 不同意）

- ***Do/Would* you agree** that we can learn from history?
- **Do you think** that we can learn from history?

Student's Answers（考生回答）

Position → State opinion（提出见解）

- **In my opinion** it can prevent us from making the same mistakes over and over again if we reflect on past actions.
- **Personally, I feel** it can prevent us from making the same mistakes over and over again if we reflect on past actions.
- **I strongly believe** it can prevent us from making the same mistakes over and over again if we reflect on past actions.
- **I am of the opinion that** it can prevent us from making the same mistakes over and over again if we reflect on past actions.
- **If you ask me** it can prevent us from making the same mistakes over and over again if we reflect on past actions.
- **To the best of my knowledge** it can prevent us from making the same mistakes over and over again if we reflect on past actions.
- **In my experience** it can prevent us from making the same mistakes over and over again if we reflect on past actions.
- **As far as I'm concerned** it can prevent us from making the same mistakes over and over again if we reflect on past actions.
- **As far as I know** it can prevent us from making the same mistakes over and over again if we reflect on past actions.
- **To my mind** it can prevent us from making the same mistakes over and over again if we reflect on past actions.

Support → Mixed strategies（综合论述）

Although this is easier said than done, history teaches us to learn from our mistakes. **That is not to say** we should dwell on our past failures all the time **but rather** work out what went wrong **so** we don't face the same problem again in the future. **And another thing**, by looking at the past it is an indicator of how far we have progressed, what we have accomplished and what still needs doing.

This support includes a **contrast**, **explanation**, **preference**, **purpose** and **extra detail**.

Identifying
确认

Examiner's Questions（主考官提问）

Question → Identifying （确认）

1. **What dangers are there in** working too much and not resting enough?
2. **What significance does** food **have** at family celebrations in your country?
3. **What right do** organisations **have** to store potentially sensitive personal data?
4. **What responsibilities do** teachers **have** to their students?
5. **What effect does** immigration **have** on the economy?
6. **What role should** the government **play** in providing health care?
7. **Could you** ***outline/identify*** the benefits of air travel?

Student's Answers（考生回答）

Position → State which ones in particular (Question 1 sample) （强调论点）

- **There are a number of risks but I'd like to point out** emotional stress.
- **There are some** dangers **but I'd like to single out** emotional stress.
- **The** ***key/main/major/prime/chief*** danger **is** emotional stress.
- **There aren't many risks but I guess I could highlight** emotional stress.

Support → Mixed strategies （综合论述）

The reason why your mental well-being often suffers **stems from the fact that** you can never turn down work. **This results in** having too many things on your plate and before you know it, you are beyond the stage where you feel you can still successfully prioritise. It's at this time you **realize** some things will go unaccomplished and **consequently** you become emotionally stressed out. **Besides**, if you don't release this pressure it'll keep building up inside until eventually you suffer from a nervous breakdown.

How + adj.
How 的提问

Examiner's Questions (主考官提问)

Question → How + adj. (How+形容词)

1. **How important is** parental supervision when kids watch TV?
2. **How concerned are you about** global deforestation?
3. **How much influence do** fashion magazines **have** on teenage girls?
4. **How effective is** the government in promoting the tourism industry in your country?
5. **How *serious/noticeable* is the problem of** illegal immigration to your country?

Student's Answers (考生回答)

Position → State degree (表明程度)

Positively high degree

1. I personally feel it's ***unbelievably/remarkably/incredibly/highly/deeply/exceptionally*** important for children to be accompanied by an adult while watching television.

Negatively high degree

2. I am ***awfully/terribly/dreadfully*** worried about the destruction of forests around the world.

Some degree

3. I believe that fashion magazines **have a *fairly/pretty/quite/moderately/rather/somewhat/reasonably* large** influence over young ladies.

Support → Mixed strategies (for Position 3) (综合性论述)

A prime example is the fact that there has been a rise in dietary problems for young women over the past few decades which **has often been associated with** the unrealistically thin images that fashion magazines promote as being beautiful. **Secondly**, consumer spending is always on the increase and that of teenage girls is no exception to this trend **as** they are often targeted by multimillion dollar advertising campaigns to buy, buy, buy everything from cosmetics to socks **in order to** be just as hot as the model in the catalogue. **All things**

considered, I am of the opinion that the fashion industry has quite a bit to answer for.

This support includes **examples**, **reasons**, **purpose** and **summary**.

IELTS

SUPERIOR SPEAKING

题库与 9 分口语范例

Test Bank with Sample Answers from Native Speakers

Test Bank with Sample Answers

Sample 1
Natural Disasters
自然灾害

Part 1 *MP3 14*

Hello, my name is (examiner's name).
What's your full name please?
Can I check your ID and passport please?
In the first part, I'd like to ask you some general questions about yourself.

Let's talk about the town or city you live in.
- Where do you live?
- What is your neighbourhood like?
- Do you get along with your neighbours?

Now I'd like to discuss the topic of friends. Is that okay?
- How much time do you spend with friends?
- Would you rather spend your free time with family or friends?
- Are you still in contact with any friends from high school?

Let's move on to music.
- What kind of music do you like?
- Can music change the way you feel?
- Have you ever been to a live concert?

Part 2

In Part 2, I will give you a topic and I'd like you to talk about it for 1-2 minutes. Before you talk, you will have one minute to think about what you are going to say. You may make some notes if you wish. Do you understand?

Topic Card

Describe a natural disaster that has occurred in your country.
You should say:
- what it was
- when it was
- what destruction it caused

and explain how it made you feel.

- Does this kind of disaster happen often in your country?
- Did it take your country a long time to recover?

Part 3

You've been talking about a natural disaster that has occurred in your country and I'd like to ask you one or two more questions related to this.
Let's consider first of all:

Natural disasters
- Comment on the effect that natural disasters have on the economy.
- Suggest some ways we can help those affected by natural disasters.
- Compare the severity of natural disasters to man made disasters.

Charities
- Outline what kind of support charities provide.
- Evaluate the effectiveness of charities.
- Agree/Disagree that volunteer work should be part of the school curriculum.

Thank you. That is the end of the speaking test.

Sample Answer 9分口语范例

SCRIPT 对话内容

The following script is of native speakers. 以下对话中的考生是母语为英语的外国人。

Part 1

Hello, my name is Robert Bowie. What's your full name please?

Sammy Ray.

OK. Can I check your ID and passport please?

Sure.

That's fine. Thank you. Now in the first part, I'd like to ask you some general questions about yourself. Let's talk about the town or city you live in. Where do you live?

I live in North London in a place called Highgate. It's very nice there actually. It's quite famous. There's a cemetery there called Highgate Cemetery and Karl Marx is buried there.

What is your neighbourhood like?

My neighbourhood is pretty nice. There's quite a lot of greenery, a few parks, a lot of good places to go out at night but otherwise it's obviously not that great but better than the north of England.

And do you get along with your neighbours?

Some of them. Some of them are rather loud. They've got pretty loud kids and they're usually quite loud at night but apart from that they're fairly friendly.

Now I'd like to discuss the topic of friends. Is that OK?

Yeah OK.

How much time do you spend with friends?

I spend quite a lot of time with friends. Whenever I have free time from work, I like to hang out with my mates. Sometimes we go to the movies or go on a trip somewhere.

Would you rather spend your free time with family or friends?

I guess I'd probably rather spend time with my friends coz my family are fairly old and boring. So I can't really go clubbing with my mum and granddad, so I'd rather spend time with my mates.

Are you still in contact with any friends from high school?

Yeah, I am, actually. A few of them, even though most of them are now in various locations. Most of them have moved out of England. They're either living in the States or other places in Europe but we stay in contact quite a lot with the Internet and Facebook.

Let's move on to music. What kind of music do you like?

I like all sorts of music really, especially opera, and classical, drum bass anything that's got a good beat to it really, especially older stuff as well.

Can music change the way you feel?

Yeah, I think so. It can also enhance the way you feel. If you're feeling like quite energetic and you listen to energising music, it can make you even more energised. On the other hand, if you listen to really calm music, it can make you feel a bit sleepy and tired sometimes.

Have you ever been to a live concert?

Yeah, I've been to quite a few live concerts. For example, probably my favourite concert I went to was Michael Jackson. It was absolutely fantastic. We liked to dance with our shirts off and do that hip rotating dances. It was very good fun.

Part 2

In Part 2, I will give you a topic and I'd like you to talk about it for one to two minutes. Before you talk, you will have one minute to think about what you are going to say. You may make some notes if you wish. Do you understand?

Yes.

Here's your pen and pencil. I'd like you to describe a natural disaster that has occurred in your country.

Well, the natural disaster that occurred in my country that springs to mind is the one that happened in a place called Boscom Bay which is in the south west of England. It was a flash flood basically. A flash flood is a very fast happening flood. It was very destructive, it destroyed a whole village called Boscom Bay, and very sad actually. Many people lost their lives, their livestock, cattle especially perished in this disaster. I think, it occurred maybe 4 or 5 years ago. As well as causing disaster to the local people, their homes were destroyed, the landscape was significantly altered. Everyone felt extremely sad because of this. It actually tends to happen quite often now maybe because of global warming. There's been an increase in the number of floodings. For example, maybe 3 years ago, there was another great flood in south west England again near a place called Chippingham. There were trees and bridges actually under water. It was impossible to drive up north. This lasted for about 3 days and actually it was quite inconvenient because I was trying to go up to the Lake District which is in the north of England. I think it took around 3 or 4 days to recover. Even after the floods had receded, they needed to remove lots of the debris from especially the motorways. There were many rocks strewn all over the place. So I think this is probably likely to increase actually. As I said global warming and climate change is causing an increase in hostile climate.

Did it take your country a long time to recover from this flash flood?

As I said, it probably took about maybe 3 days for the floods to recede but then I think emotionally people are still recovering now. You know, people who lost their lives, people who lost their pets and cows.

Part 3

OK, that's 2 minutes. Let's move on to Part 3. You've been talking about a natural disaster that has occurred in your country and I'd like to ask you one or two more general questions related to this. Let's consider first of all natural disasters. Can you comment on the effect that natural disasters have on the economy?

Well, although from one perspective, natural disasters devastate the economy to a large extent. You know businesses are destroyed, etc., therefore people lose their jobs for a period of time. However, it's also been argued that it stimulates the economy in some ways. For example, you know building contractors will be hired and it often causes an increase of investment by the government to try and help the area to develop again.

And could you suggest some ways we can help those affected by natural disasters?

Well I think first and foremost people obviously need to make sure they have somewhere to live. If they have lost their homes, sorry, they will need sufficient shelter and you know medical attention. But also quite importantly I think is, you know psychological help. People can often be rather traumatised after these kinds of events and I think some kind of counselling is often quite important.

Could you compare the severity of natural disasters to man made disasters?

Well, it's a difficult question really because you know man made disasters could be worse than natural disasters or vice versa. For example, Chernobyl which was the nuclear power plant in Russia melted down and caused and still is causing a great deal of damage to the environment and people. However, you know smaller incidents have occurred which probably aren't as devastating as say earthquakes which have happened in places around the world, you know in New Orleans the flooding, hurricanes. However, it could be argued that, you know a man made disaster is global warming. You know that is actually causing all of these natural disasters so it is difficult to actually determine where to draw the line between natural and man made disasters.

Let's talk about charities. You mentioned before ways that you could help those affected by natural disasters. Could you outline what kind of support charities provide in these times?

Well, I think in these times, mainly they would provide material support. You know as mentioned earlier maybe shelter in the form of tents, emergency supplies, medical care and possibly also counselling, I would say.

How effective do you think charities are in providing such support?

I think it's difficult to generalise. It has been argued obviously that a lot of money given to charities is often wasted on buying materials. You know expensive cars, Range Rovers to travel to certain places. Also you know that people receive high salaries from them and sometimes that the work that is actually done is not even that necessary. Maybe they decide to do some project but it takes 3 or 4 years until they can actually put that plan into action and by that time it's no longer of any use. You know, the area has different requirements so I think it depends.

OK, one last question. Would you agree or disagree that volunteer work should be part of the school curriculum?

I think if it was at the expense of more important subjects, then maybe not but I think it certainly does have its own merits. You know, it would encourage people to see the benefit of helping others to see how actually it's quite a rewarding thing in itself and maybe to open people up to the possibility of gaining some kind of satisfaction in life other than just making money for themselves.

Thank you. That is the end of the speaking test.

Sample 2
Media
媒体

Part 1 *MP3 15*

Hello, my name is (examiner's name).
What's your full name please?
Can I check your ID and passport please?
In the first part, I'd like to ask you some general questions about yourself.

Let's talk about the town or city you come from.

- Is your hometown big or small?
- What kind of jobs do people have in your hometown?
- What is your hometown famous for?

Now I'd like to ask some questions about your culture.

- What is interesting about your culture?
- What might a foreigner find difficult to understand about your culture?
- What might be considered rude in your culture?

Let's move on to TV and film.

- Do many people have cable TV in your country? Why/Why not?
- Are there many cinemas in your city?
- Do you prefer to watch a movie at home or at the movie theatre?

Part 2

In Part 2, I will give you a topic and I'd like you to talk about it for 1-2 minutes. Before you talk, you will have one minute to think about what you are going to say. You may make some notes if you wish. Do you understand?

Topic Card

Describe a newspaper you enjoy reading.
You should say:
- what the newspaper is
- what sections it has
- when and how often you read it

and express why you like it.

- Do you read any other newspapers?
- When did you first start reading this newspaper?

Part 3

You've been talking about a newspaper that you read and I'd like to ask you one or two more questions related to this. Let's consider first of all:

Newspapers
- Outline what role newspapers play in our society these days.
- Agree/Disagree that newspapers will be replaced some time in the future.
- Consider the need for news censorship.

The media
- Speculate on why the media tends to sensationalise the news.
- Evaluate how much influence the media has over young people.
- Comment on how much the media has contributed to globalisation.

Thank you. That is the end of the speaking test.

Sample Answer 9分口语范例

SCRIPT 对话内容

The following script is of native speakers. 以下对话中的考生是母语为英语的外国人。

Part 1

Hello my name is David Daffenberger. What's your full name please?

My name is Dorothy Fitzgerald.

Can I check your ID and passport please?

Sure.

In the first part, I'd like to ask you some general questions about yourself.

OK.

Let's talk about the town or city you come from. Is your hometown big or small?

My hometown is quite small actually. It's the capital of Nevada, the state that I am from. But there are only about 50,000 people there and there is only one high school.

What kind of jobs do people have in your hometown?

Well, I suppose they have jobs like every other town. There are teachers and doctors and lawyers but my hometown is special because we have casinos so lots of people work there also.

What is your hometown famous for?

Well it is famous for the casinos that are there but it's also famous because it's right next to Lake Tahoe. And Lake Tahoe is beautiful and lots of people like to go there for skiing and snowboarding in the winter.

Now I'd like to ask some questions about culture. What is interesting about your culture?

Well, since I'm American, my culture is quite famous. It's in all the movies and on TV all the time. So I guess what everybody thinks of would be baseball and American football and of course Hollywood and our movies and our music.

What might a foreigner find difficult to understand about your culture?

I suppose if they're from Asia they might find it difficult that we are so direct and many people say Americans are quite loud so some people might think it's difficult to deal with us.

What is considered rude in your culture?

Well, I'm not sure honestly about what's considered rude in my culture but in my family it was very rude to talk with food in your mouth.

OK, let's move on to TV and film. Do many people have cable TV in your country?

Oh, of course. Everybody has cable TV in America. And most people have more than 100 channels on their TV also.

Are there many cinemas in your city?

Well like I said, my hometown is very small so there were only 2 or 3 cinemas.

Do you prefer to watch a movie at home or at the movie theatre?

I definitely like going to the movie theatre more. I really love the whole experience of buying your drink and your popcorn and going with your friends and watching it on the big screen. I just saw a 3D movie, a horror movie and it was fantastic.

Part 2

In Part 2, I will give you a topic and I'd like you to talk about it for one to two minutes. Before you talk, you will have one minute to think about what you are going to say. You may make some notes if you wish. Do you understand?

Yes.

OK. Here's a pen and paper and your topic.

Thank you.

I'd like you to describe a newspaper you enjoy reading.

I would like to introduce my favourite newspaper today. It's called *The New York Times*. I didn't start reading it until I was in high school and my mum moved to New York and so when I would visit her, I would read the paper on the weekends when I was there. It has every section that normal newspapers have. It has news about international events and national, in America, events and also local news from New York. In addition, it has a wonderful travel section that has articles from all over the world and it offers perspectives that you don't get in normal newspapers. On Sundays, it has a special supplement. It has a magazine that comes with it and my favourite article is in there. It's all about language and it puts together the history of words and it explains why we say the things we do so I always read that. I only read it once a week now because I don't have much time with work and all. But when I do read it, I like to sit down at my computer because I live abroad so I obviously can't get the real paper. But I sit down at my computer and I have a nice cup of tea and I take a couple of hours to read it actually. I really enjoy catching up on all the news from my country and also the news from New York City because I think it's a fascinating city and I really wish that I can live there some day so I like reading about that. I also like seeing all the news about the travel and possible places I might take vacations in the future because usually they're places I wouldn't even think about, like going to Sri Lanka maybe or going to Bali. I've never been to these places before.

Part 3

OK, thank you. So you've been talking about a newspaper you read and I'd like to ask you one or two more questions related to this. Let's consider first of all newspapers. Outline what role newspapers play in our society these days.

Well, I think newspapers are still important despite what many people say. I think they offer different news on politics and a lot of people still depend on newspapers to get their ideas about what laws should be passed and who they should vote for. They also play an important social role. They list all the activities that you can do over the weekend with your family or friends and what concerts and other art events are coming to town.

And do you agree or disagree that newspapers will be replaced some time in the future?

You know that's hard to say. I would like to say that they cannot be replaced because I love the feel of newspapers, of having a newspaper in your hand. However, I must be realistic and say that they probably will be replaced. I think along with books and magazines people just won't need to buy the real paper products like that. They'll have their iphones or their e-readers to catch up on news with.

OK. Consider the need for news censorship.

Well, to be honest, I don't think there is a need for news censorship ever. I think that it's very wrong to not give news to people, to not give information to people that they might need. Besides that, the people that actually censor the news are usually the authorities, are usually people in power. They often censor news to make people do what they want, to make people vote a certain way, or behave in a certain way. So I think that's not fair and I think everyone has the right to know what's happening.

OK, let's move on to the media now. Speculate on why the media tends to sensationalise the news.

I believe that everyone likes to be entertained and in order to sell things, to sell newspapers or to make people watch your news channel, you have to be entertaining. Therefore you have to show pictures of people crying or of accidents and violence and people really want to see the drama, to see the violence like that. I don't know if it's because we're used to watching it on TV or in the movies and we're just used to being entertained like that, but unfortunately people are not entertained by positive news so all of the drama and the violence are shown.

Evaluate how much influence the media has over young people.

Oh, they have a lot of influence, a great deal of influence on young people. Young people love to listen to the latest music, to the pop music that everyone else likes or to follow the fashion trends. Therefore they have to look at the magazines to see what their favourite singer is wearing or what the movie stars wore at the academy awards for example, and they want to look like that. They want to look like famous people so they dress like the people they see in the media. Also if they see a celebrity is maybe interested in a new type of music or a new issue then they'll try to learn more about that. So the media, yeah, they have a lot of influence over young people.

And finally I'd like you to comment on how much the media has contributed to globalisation.

Well that's a difficult question. Let me give you an example. Coca Cola is a good example. Coca Cola is everywhere. Products like that, that you can find in any small village in Mexico or any big city in China, it's the same product, it's the same company and that's part of globalisation and the reason why people know about these products is due to the media, is due to advertising. Like I mentioned before, people follow celebrities. When celebrities endorse products, it makes people want to buy them. So advertising, I think just advertising in the media has contributed to globalisation.

Thank you. That is the end of the speaking test.

Sample 3
Food · Health
饮食 · 健康

Part 1 *MP3 16*

Hello, my name is (examiner's name).
What's your full name please?
Can I check your ID and passport please?
In the first part, I'd like to ask you some general questions about yourself.

Let's talk about what you do.
- Do you work or are you a student?
- What subjects do you study?
- Why did you choose this subject?
- What do you find difficult in your studies?

Now I'd like to ask some questions about computers.
- When did you first use a computer?
- Have computers made our lives easier?
- How can computers help you learn English?

Let's move on to health.
- What do you do to keep fit?
- What do you do when you catch a cold?
- Have you ever tried traditional Chinese medicine?

Part 2

In Part 2, I will give you a topic and I'd like you to talk about it for 1-2 minutes. Before you talk, you will have one minute to think about what you are going to say. You may make some notes if you wish. Do you understand?

Topic Card

Describe a restaurant you like.
You should say:
- what kind of food it has
- what kind of atmosphere it has
- where it is

and explain what makes it special.

- Has it been open long?
- Is it expensive?

Part 3

You've been talking about a restaurant you enjoy and I'd like to ask you one or two more questions related to this.
Let's consider first of all:

Food
- Examine the dangers of dieting.
- Identify the arguments for and against vegetarianism.
- Assess the popularity of organic food in your country.

Businesses
- Compare global to local companies.
- Identify some famous companies from your country.
- Discuss the challenges of starting your own business.

Thank you. That is the end of the speaking test.

Sample Answer 9分口语范例

SCRIPT 对话内容

The following script is of native speakers. 以下对话中的考生是母语为英语的外国人。

Part 1

Hello my name is Pauline Jones. What's your full name please?

My name is Cliff Wilson.

Can I check your ID and passport please?

Sure. Here you go.

Thank you. That's fine. Now, in this first part, I'd like to ask you some general questions about yourself. Let's talk about what you do. Do you work or are you a student?

I'm a student at the moment. I'm studying at Griffith University.

What subjects do you study?

I'm majoring in Media Studies so with media studies I'm learning about film production. We get to make movies, like short movies and documentaries and scriptwriting and also doing producing or editing, all aspects of media production.

Why did you choose this subject?

Well, when I graduated from high school, I didn't really know what I wanted to do and I thought media production sounded pretty cool. I could make movies. Then, I thought being in the movie industry, you get to meet lots of interesting people, famous people, maybe some nice actresses or some cool actors and things like that.

What do you find difficult in your studies?

Well, I think I'm more of a creative person so doing things like thinking of scripts and trying to be more creative is quite easy, but for the difficult part, it's learning all the different machines, like if you were doing editing, video editing, learning what all the different buttons do and all the different functions and how to use them effectively and correctly. It's a lot for my brain to take in, I suppose.

Now I'd like to ask some questions about computers. When did you first use a computer?

The first time I used a computer was back in primary school. I remember the school made a huge fuss out of it. When the library, when the school got its first computer, it was only one computer, it went into the library and everybody made a huge deal out of it and everybody got to use it just for about one minute.

Have computers made our lives easier?

Definitely made our lives easier. If we're talking about studies, in the past I remember still using a typewriter and when you're writing an assignment and you're making mistakes you have to, you know I can't even remember what the word is but you have to go back and then try to correct it. These days with the Internet obviously you've got functions like copying and pasting so it's very easy to produce your homework, your assignments. Obviously this is also very good for work; The fact that you can save lots of documents means that you don't have to be fumbling through paper trying to find a document that you wrote last year. You can just do a search for it and it comes up immediately.

How can computers help you learn English?

Well, there are many different functions that computers have. So I suppose for learning English, you now have CD-ROMs. There are lots of different types of CD-ROMs. So for example a dictionary can come on a CD-ROM. So it's very quick and easy to find the word that you are looking for as opposed to using a paper version of the dictionary where you have to keep turning the page until you find the correct word. With these dictionary CD-ROMs, they have lots of different functions too like a thesaurus. It also gives you exercises. You can then listen to the pronunciation. So apart from CD-ROMs, if you're talking about the Internet, there are lots of e-learning programs which will actually guide students through a whole process of learning the language.

Let's move on to health. What do you do to keep fit?

Actually, I don't do very much at all these days to keep fit. However, if I do get the chance, I like to play squash. The reason why I like to play squash is because you can start to sweat really quickly, really easily. Like once you're on the court for a couple of minutes, you start to sweat profusely just through the very active nature of the sport. So squash is definitely the best.

What do you do when you catch a cold?

Again, I do very little when I catch a cold. I like to get rid of the cold naturally so I very rarely see a doctor. I very rarely take medicine. I don't stay at home and rest. I still usually go to work and just try to sweat it out.

Have you ever tried traditional Chinese medicine?

I have actually. I like to try lots of different things so I have tried acupuncture. I have tried, I think they call it cupping, where they put the cups on your back and they suck all the oxygen out or something like that. I've tried, I don't know what the name is in English, but it's like a Chinese massage where they actually pull and push your different joints in and out of the right place. And then I've also tried the herbal medicine which usually doesn't taste very nice.

Part 2

OK. In Part 2, I'll give you a topic and I'd like you to talk about it for one to two minutes. Before you talk, you will have one minute to think about what you are going to say. You may make some notes if you wish. Do you understand?

Yes, I understand.

OK. Here's some paper and a pencil for making notes and here is your topic. I'd like you to describe a restaurant you like.

I actually go to lots of different restaurants quite regularly but because I'm not a huge fan of food, I don't actually have like a favourite restaurant. But if I have to talk about one, I'd actually like to mention the regular place I go to which is a restaurant slash lounge bar. The name of the restaurant is called 2046 and it's in the eastern district of Taipei. The reason why I like it is because it's a very relaxed atmosphere. You can sit outside. There's an inside area and outside area. When you sit outside, you get to see lots of people walking by because it's a shopping area also. There's a bar there so you can have a few drinks if you want with your friends. Then they've also got lots of bar food so you can have everything from just your average French fries to a clam soup and to something a bit more substantial like some kind of rice or noodle dish. The atmosphere there is very good. I like the atmosphere there. It's relaxing. You get to see many people walking in and out. They play music. It's not too loud. It's just background music but it is more upbeat music. It's like the DJ music that you hear like in nightclubs and things like that. And the reason why it's special is because I like to go there. There's probably no real reason that it's really special but I think I've just got used to going there and I'm pretty lazy to think about any other possible places I can go to so that's what makes it special. It's my regular restaurant slash lounge bar.

Has it been open long?

There's been like a restaurant there for a long time but it was under different management before. I think under the current name of 2046, it might only be a couple of years old but I'm not entirely sure.

Part 3

OK, thank you. You've been talking about a restaurant you enjoy and I'd like to ask you one or two more questions related to this. Let's consider first of all food. What do you think the dangers of dieting are?

These days, especially with women, there's a lot of pressure on them to diet to make sure that they have a slim body; something that reflects the types of bodies that they see in magazines and on TV by famous models and TV stars. So that sometimes means that females might diet to the extreme and then they might not eat for a few days or they only drink one kind of juice or they eat one type of food. So obviously this is not healthy for the body. So although they might get thinner, it doesn't make them healthier.

OK. What about vegetarianism? What are the arguments for and against vegetarianism?

That's a good question, interesting question. I was actually a vegetarian for over 7 years and I found the good things were that I felt I had more energy. Like I didn't feel, especially after eating a big meal of meat, you kind of feel really full and you don't have any energy left, you just wanna go to sleep. Whereas with vegetarianism, you don't actually get that full so you feel like you always have energy. However, I don't think it gives you enough energy in the long term so I thought after a few years of being vegetarian, I actually felt that my body was weaker. It wasn't as strong in lots of different ways. So for example I felt I used to slouch more. I didn't sit up straight. I didn't stand straight because I don't think I had the strength in the bottom of my back. But obviously there are other reasons why you should be vegetarian. So for example it might be to protect animals because you might be very environmentally, want to be environmentally friendly. It might be for religious reasons because you don't want to kill any animals. But I think the main point is that you should try to lead a healthy diet where you have lots of energy and you don't get sick.

What about organic food? Is that popular in your country?

I think it is quite popular. Obviously organic food has been around for a while now and it is much more popular than in the past. I think organic food is probably more popular with the very health-conscious or those who are vegetarian and they don't want to be taking any food that might have been treated with pesticides. It is more popular than in the past but I wouldn't say it's mainstream.

OK, let's talk about businesses. Can you compare global and local companies?

Sure. Global companies, as the name suggests, they work on an international scale which often means they have more resources at their disposal compared to local companies. However, sometimes global companies can be a little bit too general so the advantage that local companies have is that they can focus on their particular market, target this market and make sure that the products that they are providing or the services that they are providing actually meet the needs of their local market.

OK. What are some famous companies from your country?

Some famous companies? I don't think there are that many. There must be some famous companies, for example QANTAS. It's an airline company from Australia. I think everybody has heard of QANTAS. I think it's because they haven't had any plane crashes and it was made famous in the movie with Tom Cruise and Dustin Hoffman which I can't remember. Apart from QANTAS people have probably heard of Foster's which is the beer but actually nobody drinks that in Australia. And then I can't think of any more famous Australian companies, I'm sorry.

That's OK. What about starting your own business? What would the challenges be of starting your own business?

First of all you need the capital. If you don't have enough money, you might have enough money to start the company but then obviously at the beginning you're not going to be making a lot of money. So you have to have enough cash or financial reserves to keep going through the first couple of years. So money is probably the biggest problem. Then also at the beginning you probably don't have that many staff so you have to do a lot of things yourself. It probably includes doing everything from the small jobs to the big decision-making. So you'll be working, I'm sure, long hours to ensure that your business does become successful. And then also being small when you first start out trying to compete with your major competitors who are already established, have got a reputation already, have got probably lots of money to support them.

OK, thank you. That is the end of the speaking test.

Sample 4
Environment
环境

Part 1 MP3 17

Hello, my name is (examiner's name).
What's your full name please?
Can I check your ID and passport please?
In the first part, I'd like to ask you some general questions about yourself.

Let's talk about your job or studies.
- What do you do?
- What don't you enjoy about your studies?
- What are your study plans?
- Is there anything else you would like to study?

Now I'd like to talk about festivals and holidays.
- Which festival from your country is your favourite?
- How do you usually spend your holidays?
- Would you like to have longer holidays?

Let's move on to food.
- Can you cook?
- Would you rather stay at home or go out to eat?
- Can you describe some traditional food from your country?

Part 2

In Part 2, I will give you a topic and I'd like you to talk about it for 1-2 minutes. Before you talk, you will have one minute to think about what you are going to say. You may make some notes if you wish. Do you understand?

Topic Card

> Describe a place of natural beauty in your country.
> You should say:
> ■ where it is
> ■ what you can do there
> ■ when the best time to go is
> and explain what makes it so attractive.

■ Would you like to go there again?
■ Do many people know about this place?

Part 3

You've been talking about a place of natural beauty in your country and I'd like to ask you one or two more general questions related to this.
Let's consider first of all:

The environment
■ Compare the importance of increasing the standard of living to protecting the environment.
■ Assess who is more responsible for protecting the environment—individuals or governments.
■ Suggest some alternative energy sources that can be developed more.

Beauty
■ Evaluate how important a beautiful appearance is in order to be successful in life.
■ Justify the need for cosmetic surgery.
■ Compare how males and females have different ideas on beauty.

Thank you. That is the end of the speaking test.

Sample Answer 9分口语范例

SCRIPT 对话内容

The following script is of native speakers. 以下对话中的考生是母语为英语的外国人。

Part 1

Hello my name is Damien Lyons. What's your full name please?

My name is Frederick Elliot Monk.

Can I check your ID and passport please?

Sure.

Thank you. That's fine. In the first part, I'd like to ask you some general questions about yourself. Let's talk about your job or studies. What do you do?

Well, I'm a songwriter actually at the moment. I compose scores for short films and also jingles for radio and TV but I found that even though the job is creative and rewarding, I found the income to be not incredibly dependable. So at the moment I'm doing a master's degree in financial engineering and I hope to be running a hedge fund in the near future.

What don't you enjoy about your studies?

I find that there's lots of repetition and in lots of the management subjects there's, it feels like, there's common sense which has been given very big scientific names and I feel the regurgitation of that information bores me a lot.

What are your study plans?

My study plans are to finish my master's degree and after the master's, hopefully never again. Maybe the odd course, maybe when I'm 70, I may take up fine art, start painting.

Is there anything else you would like to study?

Yes, just the fine arts when I'm 70, when I grow old. I think it will be a, it's a romantic picture moving to an island somewhere after my hedge fund did really well.

Good. Now I'd like to talk to you about festivals and holidays. Which festival from your country is your favourite?

We have a festival, a marvellous festival every year which centres around the making of sausage and from my country there's a vast array of sausages but of course sausage being the centre point of it. There's lots of music and theatre that comes around at the same time. That festival just because I guess it has strange roots but it's also become a very big cultural affair. That's definitely my favourite.

How do you usually spend your holidays?

My holidays are usually as close to the ocean as possible. I used to be a lifesaver when I was a teenager and I enjoyed long-distance swims as well as bodysurfing so I'd spend as much time at the beach as I can.

Would you like to have longer holidays?

Of course! Who wouldn't want to have longer holidays? My plan for the hedge fund is so I can retire by the time I am 35.

Let's move on to food. Can you cook?

I can cook. I do, yes. I don't have the patience to read from a cook book and I usually don't use the same set of ingredients twice but I have fun.

Would you rather stay at home or go out to eat?

I very often like to stay at home. My girlfriend is quite a picky eater and she loves going out, so unfortunately I have to spend almost all my money on her going out as often as I can. I think my food's pretty good.

Can you describe some traditional food from your country?

Well talking about the sausage, I have to come back to the sausage as far as that's, well I'll leave the sausage. I've spoken about the sausage enough. But my country is well known for cooking very thick pieces of steak—not very interesting but wonderful.

<u>Part 2</u>

In Part 2, I will give you a topic and I'd like you to talk about it for one to two minutes. Before you talk, you will have one minute to think about what you are going to say. You may make some notes if you wish. Do you understand?

Yes.

Here's your pen and paper and here's your topic card. I'd like you to describe a place of natural beauty in your country.

The place that springs to mind is Cape Town which is in my city. It's a wonderfully impressive mountain because it rises so steeply, very close to the shore. It's almost one and a half kilometres high, less than 3 kilometres from the shore. It's got the city wrapped all around it. There was some legislation that was passed quite a few years ago that one is not allowed to build any structure above a certain line on the mountain so it's a well-preserved area in the middle of the city; so wherever you are in the city if you walk for 20 minutes you'll be in the mountain. It's great. What you can do there is, well I guess sightseeing is first. There's a cable car that goes up the mountain which draws a wealth of Asian and European tourists and this cable car actually rotates so that you're given a 360 degree view without effectively changing your spot on the floor. And once you get to the top there are some hiking trails and of course the top it's, there are so many ways to get lost. I've spent many hours in valleys and in fog trying to find my way back. It's exhilarating, kind of scary but exhilarating. I think the best time to go to Table Mountain would definitely be in the summer because the winter months are rainy and very, very cold whereas the summer is dry with blue skies. It's gorgeous. It's a very Mediterranean type of climate and the kind of flora which one encounters there is also seen in the Mediterranean. But even though the flora looks Mediterranean, it's a whole genus of its own called Fynbos. And I guess if you're in any way interested in botany, it would be a wonderful place to go. There's almost a quarter of million plant species there which are not found anywhere else in the world.

Part 3

Let's move on to Part 3. You've been talking about a place of natural beauty in your country and I'd like to ask you one or two more general questions related to this. Let's consider first of all the environment. Could you compare the importance of increasing the standard of living to protecting the environment?

Well, I don't think those two concepts are mutually exclusive. I think the enhancement of our environment will definitely raise our standard of living also. At the moment if people think that a high standard of living is having all the mod cons, having all your creature comforts while breathing dirty air, then people are deluding themselves. I think finding a good, clean way to live is very important for human kind.

I would also like to know, in your opinion, who is more responsible for protecting the environment, is it individuals or governments?

I think the onus lies with individuals but I think it lies with them in supporting what governments have decided as to being a game plan for the country. I think that people should express their feelings and I think these feelings should be codified and they should be summarised and that should be the basis for legislation for the country and it's up to people to support that legislation if it does come to pass.

Could you suggest some alternative energy sources that can be developed more?

I think wind energy in the areas where there is lots of wind is an untapped resource. I think that tide energy is also a very interesting field as that generally is, it's an absolute plenitude of power which is completely unharnessed at present.

Let's move on to talk about beauty. Could you tell me how important a beautiful appearance is in order to be successful in life?

I don't think it's really important to have stunning good looks to do well. I think it's important to be presentable and I think it's important to not be off-putting. I don't think your looks need to be a severe help to you but they also should not, your appearance should not be a hindrance either.

Do you think that there is a need for cosmetic surgery?

I think if it's reconstructive, I think yes. I do know that there are cases where people get addicted to cosmetic surgery and lose sight of themselves through all that. I think that's destructive but there are definitely some cases in the world where people do need help to have as enjoyable life as possible.

One last question. Could you compare how males and females have different ideas on beauty?

That's a tough question. It's different if you think about how ladies might see themselves or how they might see men and how men might see themselves and how they might see ladies. I think if you're looking for a possible mate, then maybe... I know lots of guys who don't take care of themselves but they do expect whoever they're courting to be extremely beautiful. I'm not sure. Well actually as far as spending money on cosmetics is concerned, I'm a little bit of a metrosexual and I do like all the lotions and exfoliants and such.

Thank you. That is the end of the speaking test.

Sample 5
Law
法律

Part 1 *MP3 18*

Hello, my name is (examiner's name).
What's your full name please?
Can I check your ID and passport please?
In the first part, I'd like to ask you some general questions about yourself.

Let's talk about what you do.
- Do you work or are you a student?
- What kind of organisation do you work for?
- Are you happy you decided to do this kind of work?

Now I'd like to talk about art galleries and museums.
- Do you like to visit art galleries and museums?
- What can you learn from visiting art galleries and museums?
- Should schools take students to visit art galleries and museums?

Let's move on to talk about gardens.
- Do many people have gardens in your country?
- Why do some people like gardening?
- Have you ever grown flowers, vegetables or plants before?

Part 2

In Part 2, I will give you a topic and I'd like you to talk about it for 1-2 minutes. Before you talk, you will have one minute to think about what you are going to say. You may make some notes if you wish. Do you understand?

Topic Card

Describe a law in your country that you think is fair.
You should say:
■ what the law is
■ when the law was made
■ why it was made
and explain why you think it is fair.

■ Do other people like this law?
■ Do you think this law may change in the future?

Part 3

You've been talking about a law in your country you think is fair and I'd like to ask you one or two more general questions related to this.
Let's consider first of all:

Law related jobs
■ Compare the benefits of being a police officer with those of a lawyer.
■ Identify the qualities needed to be a good police officer.
■ Assess whether police officers have adequate power and resources to do their jobs effectively in your country.

Breaking laws
■ Consider whether most people in your country obey the law most of the time.
■ Identify times when it might be OK to break the law.
■ Agree/Disagree that the punishment for breaking a law in your country is tough enough.

Thank you. That is the end of the speaking test.

Sample Answer 9分口语范例

SCRIPT 对话内容

The following script is of native speakers. 以下对话中的考生是母语为英语的外国人。

Part 1

Hello my name is Nicole Brigants. What's your full name please?

Johnson Gerald.

OK, Johnson, can I check your ID and passport please? OK, thank you. That's fine. In the first part, I'd like to ask you some general questions about yourself. Let's talk about what you do. Do you work or are you a student?

I work and I'm also a student. I study Chinese in Taipei in the university here. I've only studied for about 4 months and I've also been working here.

What kind of organisation do you work for?

I work for a design company. I mainly design brochures for travel agents and also for tour agencies for tourists who come here to Taiwan.

Are you happy you decided to do this kind of work?

Actually yeah, I'm quite happy. It gives me a lot of satisfaction doing this job. I get to travel to many places, meet many people and I enjoy doing graphic design, so yeah.

Now I'd like to talk about art galleries and museums. Do you like to visit art galleries and museums?

Yes I do actually. There's a lot of overlap with my work. Not so much with older art but with modern contemporary art there is. I tend to go quite often maybe on the weekends to see new exhibitions and I am a member of various art forms.

What can you learn from visiting art galleries and museums?

I think obviously you can learn a lot about purely aesthetic things but you can also learn about what people were thinking in the period in which they were producing the art. For example people would often create art which had a connection. For example a religious connection at the time if you look at medieval paintings, most of it is, in Europe, connected to Christianity, religious symbolism especially.

Should schools take students to visit art galleries and museums?

Yes, I think it's good to take students to visit art galleries and museums. It gives them a broader education. If students just focus on the purely academic subjects, then I think it limits their thinking somewhat and I think the arts can actually inspire the academic subjects as well.

Let's move on to talk about gardens. Do many people have gardens in your country?

Actually yes and as a matter of fact many people do have gardens in my country. This is probably because this is part of our culture. It's very green and rains a fair bit. There's quite a lot of opportunity to do gardening.

Why do some people like gardening?

Well, I think there are a number of reasons. Probably one is that it's a good way to pass time especially for older people. It's actually seen as relatively good exercise; bending down and standing up. It's not too intense but I think it's quite enjoyable and can be quite calming.

Have you ever grown flowers, vegetables or plants before?

Well when I was younger, my mother used to grow a few garlics and onions but personally I am more preferable to asparagus, apples, the odd bit of lettuce here and there. But I don't have that much time anymore; so maybe when I'm older, I'll go back to gardening.

Part 2

In Part 2, I'll give you a topic and I'd like you to talk about it for one to two minutes. Before you talk, you will have one minute to think about what you are going to say. You may make some notes if you wish. Do you understand?

Yes.

Here's some paper and a pencil for making notes and here's your topic. I'd like you to describe a law in your country that you think is fair.

OK, today I'd like to describe a law in my country that I think that is fair. So this law is actually prohibition of capital punishment. I think the last person to have been lawfully killed in Britain was somewhere in the early 20th century maybe 1980. I'm not entirely sure but it was sometime around then. So yeah, capital punishment means that you are killed for certain crimes so for example maybe murder, crimes committed against the state, high treason and so forth. I think this was made for a number of reasons. I think one reason is that it was decided that actually nobody has the right to take life even if they, themselves have taken life coz in the end this makes you no better than the perpetrator. Secondly I think the other problem is that one can never be 100% sure that someone is guilty or not. For example, there maybe a great amount of evidence to point to the fact that, say, someone did commit murder but then there could be some evidence which actually proves otherwise which just was not recovered. So I think it was also made out of concern that if someone was convicted of having committed a crime and wasn't guilty and in turn was killed for their crimes which they didn't commit, I think that's a quite terrible thing to happen. So I think it's fair. You know, instead now, people maybe have life imprisonment where you know you have to maybe serve their country in other ways. So in my opinion this is a good law. There are countries where this isn't the case and I think it's a shame. On the other hand, it could be said that capital punishment is a better deterrent for people committing crimes in the first place, so you can argue either way.

<u>Part 3</u>

You've been talking about a law in your country you think is fair and I'd like to ask you one or two more general questions related to this. Let's consider first of all law related to jobs. Can you compare the benefits of being a police officer with those of a lawyer?

Well the first thing that springs to mind, the main benefit I think of being a lawyer is that it's seen to be a very high-paying job. For those I think of being a police officer is probably not so high-paying unless of course obviously in some countries the police officers are known to take large bribes so that maybe quite advantageous actually in some places. I also think being a police officer requires you to get your hands a bit more dirty; maybe use physical force to restrain criminals, maybe be faced with very difficult situations as well.

Can you identify the qualities needed to be a good police officer?

I think to be a good police officer you'd probably have to be fairly grounded. You know you'd need to be able to be exposed to various difficulties, challenging circumstances and still be able to remain firm, still be able to abide by the law even if say personally you didn't agree with it entirely. Obviously I think you need to be quite clear thinking, maybe also quite strong you know in case you had to defend yourself or other people.

Can you tell me in your country do police officers have adequate power and resources to do their jobs effectively?

That's quite a challenging question. I think that the problem nowadays is that there are more and more laws being given which actually restrict the police from doing various things. On the other hand, the government has also been seen to be overriding some of these say human rights. For example, in my country they now have certain what they call terror laws and this enables the police to take someone into custody for a period of time without having a just cause or without having any kind of trial whatsoever, so in some sense this enables them to say prevent a crime which they may think is going to happen but which they can't prove. So I think they do have some powers but on the other hand I think this could still be improved and also made a bit fairer.

Do you think that most people in your country obey the law most of the time?

I think most people don't commit the most serious crimes such as murder. However I think a number of people try to avoid paying certain taxes. They won't declare all their income for example. I think that's quite a widespread practice. I think also things like underage drinking, maybe driving without having the correct insurance. At least until a short time ago it was quite a fairly widely spread practice but I think the government is now clamping down on this. They are introducing measures to prevent these kinds of things.

So are these times when it might be OK to break the law?

I suppose, now and then, it's OK. You know, it depends. If the government has a way of tracking you then obviously it's not OK. Whether your conscious, sorry your conscience allows you to do it as well is another question. I think it depends really. We need to think about the repercussions, the consequences and our intention for breaking the law if we need to.

So do you feel that the punishment for breaking laws in your country is tough enough?

Well as I mentioned before we don't have the death penalty and I think there's just cause for that but I do think that people don't really seem to be so concerned about going to prison. For example life, well it has been argued that life is often quite comfortable in prison. You know prisoners have television. They have games rooms. They can actually have a fair bit of entertainment. They can even receive an education which some people would say you know is in fact rewarding them for their crimes. On the other hand, it's also seen as a way of re-educating them. You know maybe the reason that people turn to crime was because they didn't have any opportunity to do anything else so I think this is a good thing to re-educate them. Whether it should be harsher or not, I don't know, it's arguable.

OK, thank you very much. That is the end of the speaking test.

Sample 6
Charity
慈善

Part 1 *MP3 19*

Hello, my name is (examiner's name).
What's your full name please?
Can I check your ID and passport please?
In the first part, I'd like to ask you some general questions about yourself.

Let's talk about what you do.
- Do you work or are you a student?
- How did you get this job?
- Is it easy to get this kind of job?
- Did your studies prepare you for this job?

Let's talk about birthdays.
- What do people usually do on their birthdays in your country?
- What did you do on your last birthday?
- Is it important to celebrate birthdays?

I'd like to talk about evenings now.
- What do you usually do in the evening?
- What do you like to do if you go out in the evening?
- Are there many things to do in the evenings in your city?

Part 2

In Part 2, I will give you a topic and I'd like you to talk about it for 1-2 minutes. Before you talk, you will have one minute to think about what you are going to say. You may make some notes if you wish. Do you understand?

Topic Card

Describe a time when you helped someone.
You should say:
- who you helped
- when you helped him/her
- how you helped

and express how you felt about helping this person.

- Do you often like to help people?

Part 3

You've been talking about a time you helped someone and I'd like to ask you one or two more general questions related to this.
Let's consider first of all:

Volunteer work
- Suggest some types of volunteer work that you can do for your community.
- Agree/Disagree that children should be encouraged to do volunteer work.
- Identify what problems may arise from unpaid volunteer work.

Charities
- Evaluate the effectiveness of charities in helping those in need.
- Discuss the different forms of aid that charities offer.
- Compare the types of aid provided by charities to those of governments in times of crises (e.g. natural disasters).

Thank you. That is the end of the speaking test.

Sample Answer 9分口语范例

SCRIPT 对话内容

The following script is of native speakers. 以下对话中的考生是母语为英语的外国人。

Part 1

Hello, my name is Bradley Evans. What's your full name please?

I'm Harold Waterson.

Can I check your ID and passport please? That's fine. Thank you. In the first part, I'd like to ask you some general questions about yourself. Let's talk about what you do. Do you work or are you a student?

I was a student until last year so I'm quite new in the job market. I'd really enjoyed my university years and I was a little apprehensive about going into the corporate world. But I did find a job quite easily. I'm a technical writer for a software firm.

How did you get this job?

I got a lead through a cousin of mine who's been in the industry for quite a while. The interview process was quite strange as this company is full of mavericks and they look for interesting facets of one's personality.

Is it easy to get this kind of job?

I think it might be if you're motivated but you also need some luck to find the right position at the right time. I was fortunate to not be tied up in studies and also I almost went travelling at the time when my cousin contacted me with this possible job.

Did your studies prepare you for this job?

Not at all. I wanted to study commerce initially because I thought it would be a safe option which I found very, very boring by the end of my second year but I finished the third. I was mostly prepared for this job by following what my interests were and I was really interested in computers from a young age.

Let's talk about birthdays. What do people usually do on their birthdays in your country?

In my country there's a very big barbecue culture. So most birthdays, I guess well most festive times are spent outside, lots of food, lots of friends. I struggle to trust people if they don't enjoy food. So I think most birthdays are big meals with friends and family.

What did you do on your last birthday?

Well, I was lucky enough to take a trip to Bali with my really sweet Brazilian girlfriend and she took me out to dinner at the Japanese restaurant. It was wonderful.

Is it important to celebrate birthdays?

I think it is, I think it is. I'm not sure that gift giving is as important as many people make it out to be. I'm not a huge fan of merchandising as a concept but I do enjoy celebrating life and I think having a birthday is a good reason for that.

I'd like to talk about evenings now. What do you usually do in the evening?

Well in the evenings, after I finish work, seeing as I'm still new to it, I'm generally quite tired. I enjoy watching sitcoms, some entertainment which wouldn't be too cerebral. And I also love the films of Matthew McCounagh. Even though they are mainstream and they're slightly cheesy, there's something about, I don't know, the casting or the scriptwriting that always interests me.

What do you like to do if you go out in the evening?

When I go out in the evening, I usually start off by having dinner with some friends. I am a big fan of bluegrass music. So if there ever is any in the town I am staying in, I really love the sound of the fiddle and banjo together and after that I am properly primed for some clubbing.

Are there many things to do in the evenings in your city?

There are. There's a vast array of cuisine. And also as far as the live music is concerned I think I'm a fan of bluegrass because the range of bluegrass musicians has expanded dramatically over the last year or so.

Part 2

Let's move on to Part 2. I will give you a topic and I'd like you to talk about it for one to two minutes. Before you talk, you will have one minute to think about what you are going to say. You may make some notes if you wish. Do you understand?

Yes, I understand.

OK, here's your paper and pen and here's your topic. I'd like you to describe a time when you helped someone.

Well, there was this one time when I was cycling on a mountain pass near my home where I ran across these two German cycle tourists who were in dire straits as the lady's crank had fallen off her bicycle. The name of mountain pass is, well translated from my mother tongue, the heights of hell. It's an unforgiving place and quite difficult to escape from if you don't have the means. Anyway so I cycled back to my home and had to borrow a car from a friend which took a while and after a couple of hours I drove all the way back up to the mountain pass and I couldn't find these people. They said they would wait for me but I guess it took too long and they had to move on so we had to go through to one of the side roads which turned out to be the original route and we tracked them down. It took hours and hours but they were very grateful to see us and we loaded their cars into the back, sorry we loaded their bicycles into the back of my car and we drove all the way down the mountain. And I hosted them at my place for four days and even though at the time it looked like we didn't have much in common coz they were 50 something and I was 19. Klaus and Edith have become great friends of mine and lots of their cyclist friends from Germany have come over to stay with me and I have also gone over to Germany on more than one occasion to visit them. I've become great friends with their children also.

Do you often like to help people?

I do. I think it's a very important thing that what goes around, comes around mantra is a good one to live by as often as I can. It's sometimes a bit difficult if you live in a big city like I do now where people sort of become more cellular in their existence and don't connect with others as often as they should.

Part 3

Let's move on to Part 3. We've been talking about a time you helped someone and I'd like to ask you one or two more general questions related to this. Let's talk about volunteer work. Could you suggest some types of volunteer work that you can do for your community.

In my community, there's a great shortage of low cost housing and there's a group of young architects and church groups who have combined to make houses with a method that's called hay bale construction where you take clay and pack it around and compact it around hay bales to make what is a very sturdy, insulating and fireproof shelter and also quite inexpensive. So I spent two summers as a student helping to build houses with these people and it's wonderful coz the whole community will pull together. It's almost like an Amish barn-raising but it's a slightly more diverse crowd that will help to build these houses. I did that for two summers and I wish I could go back but I'm not living in the same city anymore. I think that was worthwhile; building an abode for someone.

Do you agree or disagree that children should be encouraged to do volunteer work?

Definitely, definitely. I think having financial or economic gain be the be all and end all of someone's existence is a terrible state of affairs and if children can be taught that it's important and very gratifying to give to your community, it's a wonderful lesson to learn. We actually had some young children who were part of the clay mixing part of the, the clay mixing sector of the hay bale house building project. That was fun. They had a great time. The kids loved getting dirty.

Sure. Could you identify what problems, if any, may arise from unpaid volunteer work?

Like the country where I come from where there isn't a whole lot of economic prosperity across the board, it is a problem where people are sort of depended upon to do these volunteer jobs but then without the remuneration there are some feelings of subtle distain I guess will creep in over some time. I for one, I felt like my job became quite specialised and when I had to leave I felt extremely guilty about leaving the rest of the team in the lurch and I would have liked to stay on but it was just, from an economic perspective, impossible.

Let's move on to talk about charities. Could you evaluate the effectiveness of charities in helping those in need?

That depends completely on the oversight of the charity. My lovely lady lived in South East Asia for a while and she witnessed first hand how many of the non-governmental organisations received blind funding with little oversight and so there was a lot of waste where they could have been a lot of positive influence on the community. If I look at the budget for our hay bale houses which was incredibly low, the amount of good that we did for the community was wonderful and I think that was mostly because the management and the oversight from the government in this sense was very thorough and well thought through.

Could you discuss the different forms of aid that charities offer?

Well there's just very direct financial aid of course which I don't think is a good thing and then there's other projects like the Peace Corps from America which very often they'll send people with some other philanthropist background into many parts of the world which turns out to be not so much aid but sort of a public relations exercise for the country that sends out those people.

OK, one last question Harold. Could you compare the types of aid provided by charities to those of governments in times of crises so say for example natural disasters?

Well it has to compare the readiness of governments in this regard. If you look at the recent bombings in India, the government there had a terribly slow response rate because there was no preparedness for that. I think often with charities because the problems that they're dealing with are more chronic than acute, the charities could have a better forecast of what they would be able to do. I feel that in times of crises, it depends completely on the situation and where the disaster happens and the government and their readiness is the deciding factor.

Thank you. That is the end of the speaking test.

Sample 7
Photography
摄影，照相

Part 1 *MP3 20*

Hello, my name is (examiner's name).
What's your full name please?
Can I check your ID and passport please?
In the first part, I'd like to ask you some general questions about yourself.

Let's talk about where you live.
- Do you live in a house or a flat?
- What does your house/flat look like?
- Does your house/flat have a view?
- How is your house decorated?

I'd like to discuss the Internet.
- How did you learn to use the Internet?
- What do you like about the Internet?
- What don't you like about the Internet?

Now let's move on to keeping fit.
- Do you exercise?
- Are there any fitness facilities near where you live?
- Should all students do sport at school?

Part 2

In Part 2, I will give you a topic and I'd like you to talk about it for 1-2 minutes. Before you talk, you will have one minute to think about what you are going to say. You may make some notes if you wish. Do you understand?

Topic Card

Describe a photo you have seen. You should say: ■ who took it ■ when it was taken ■ what you can see in the photo and explain what you like about it.

■ Have many people seen this photo?
■ Do you often take photos?

Part 3

You've been talking about a photo you have seen and I'd like to ask you one or two more general questions related to this. Let's consider first of all:

Photography
■ Consider why some people do not like to be photographed.
■ Compare the differences between photos and paintings.
■ Assess the popularity of built-in cameras in mobile phones.

Pictures in the media
■ Outline the benefits of using photos and illustrations in the printed media.
■ Agree/Disagree that media's use of pictures in newspapers has increased since you were a child.
■ Consider whether the media use pictures appropriately when reporting the news.

Thank you. That is the end of the speaking test.

Sample Answer 9分口语范例

SCRIPT 对话内容

The following script is of native speakers. 以下对话中的考生是母语为英语的外国人。

Part 1

Hello, my name is Duncan Fitzgerald. What's your full name please?

My name is Janice Armstrong.

Can I check your ID and passport please?

Sure.

In the first place, I'd like to ask you some general questions about yourself. Let's talk about where you live. Do you live in a house or a flat?

I live in a flat. I live in a big city so naturally I live in a flat or an apartment.

What does your house or flat look like?

My flat is, it's quite small but it has 2 bedrooms, a living room, a kitchen and a bathroom and a huge balcony. We like to have barbecues on our balcony in the summer.

And is there a good view from this balcony?

There is from one side. From one side of the balcony you can see Taipei 101 and at night especially, it looks beautiful; but from the other side you just see more buildings.

And how is your house decorated?

We have mostly photos on our wall, photos that we took of our last vacation. We went cycling in California and otherwise we have some pictures from Thailand that we bought last year.

Oh OK. Well, now I'd like to discuss the Internet. How did you learn to use the Internet?

I taught myself if I remember right. That was a long time ago. I guess I was in high school and my mum bought a computer for me and I just played around with it until I figured it out.

And what do you like about the Internet?

Well, unfortunately I don't use the Internet as often as most people. I don't like to sit at home and surf the web as they say. I mostly like it to communicate with my family that's far away and to get the latest news.

So what don't you like about the Internet?

I don't like that, those social networking sites like Facebook and those sites. I think they make it too easy to waste time. I don't like that.

OK and now let's move on to keeping fit. Do you exercise?

I do in fact exercise. I go jogging at least 3 times a week and the other days usually I go hiking or swimming sometimes.

Are there any fitness facilities near where you live?

There are. I have a nice, big gym near my house. It's two blocks away. It's quite large actually. There are three floors so it's never too crowded.

And do you think all students at school should do sport?

I think they should yeah. It's, even if you're not athletic or you don't consider yourself an athletic person, there are still individual sports that are enjoyable like swimming and, or golf or something. I think sports are important just to get outside and exercise a bit.

Part 2

OK now let's move on to Part 2. In this part, I will give you a topic and I'd like you to talk about it for one to two minutes. Before you talk, you will have one minute to think about what you are going to say. You may make some notes if you wish. Do you understand?

Yes.

OK, great. Here's a pen and paper and here's your topic. Describe a photo you have seen.

I'm going to tell you about a photo I saw yesterday actually. I saw it on the wall of a restaurant I went to and I thought it was really interesting. It was a picture from the 1920s of a group of cyclists that were doing the Tour de France. It had a group of cyclists in it. I think it featured a group of maybe 10 guys. It's black and white of course because it's from the 1920s and they're all on bicycles and it looks like they're moving. They're getting ready to climb a big mountain and they all have their cycling tubes, their extra tubes around their shoulders and the interesting thing, the thing that people take notice of when they see it is that the guys in front are handing cigarettes to each other and you wouldn't think today that somebody can do this race and smoke cigarettes. But back then they thought that smoking actually helped their respiration, their breathing so they would smoke cigarettes before they had to climb the big mountains. I actually don't know who took it. I think it was maybe in *TIME* magazine or something but it's so old. It didn't have a name on it so I don't know who took it. I like it because it shows I think a very interesting contrast in the sport between now and back then. I like the idea that, sort of any man or woman could decide to do this race and it didn't seem like you had to like train or prepare. You just, sort of got on a bike and left and started going up a mountain and today we think of it as being this gruelling, difficult, amazing race that, and people take drugs to do it. They take steroids to prepare themselves and I don't know it seems like maybe all the fun is taken out of it. Whereas back then it seems, in the picture at least, it looks like people just decided to sort of have an adventure, to have a journey and go out and take a bicycle ride.

Part 3

OK, good job. So we've been talking about a picture which you find interesting so now let's talk about photography. Consider why some people do not like to be photographed.

Well some people don't think they're very photogenic so they don't feel like they look good in a photograph. Like my mum for example, she smiles the same way in every picture. She always looks the same so she doesn't like to have her picture taken.

And compare the differences between photos and paintings.

Well, I personally prefer photos as a piece of art to buy coz they seem more real to me whereas paintings, paintings can be more imaginative I suppose. Paintings can be about fantasy or things that aren't actually there like Salvador Dali for example. Whereas photos you can't really change them too much. They have to be something in front of you.

And assess the popularity of built-in cameras in mobile phones.

Wow, yeah people love cameras in their mobile phones. They take pictures constantly. I think it's, I don't think it's too positive actually because often people don't look where they're going. They just sort of stand in the middle of the sidewalk and take a picture of a tree or a bus stop or something that's not actually worth taking a picture of. So I don't think that they should be as popular as they are.

Now let's move into pictures in the media. Outline the benefits of using photos and illustrations in the printed media.

Well, they definitely make newspapers more exciting. I don't think anyone would buy a newspaper if there was nothing but black and white words on the cover of it. I think using pictures of, to demonstrate what people really look like or how they felt during the story, like if there was an earthquake and to show how the victims are living now. It can really make stories feel more real to you.

Media's use of pictures in newspapers has increased since you were a child, do you agree or disagree?

I don't remember much about newspapers when I was a child. I well, I'm not that old so I don't think it's changed that much so I guess I disagree. I think newspapers use the same amount of pictures and well actually magazines use more pictures these days definitely. When you get a magazine the first, well women's magazines, the first 20 pages of it are all advertising and pictures, so that's probably different.

OK and finally consider whether the media use pictures appropriately when reporting the news.

Well, as I said there are ways to use them appropriately to make stories seem more real to the audience or to the readers such as showing the effects of a disaster like an earthquake or a typhoon or a mudslide maybe to show what happened to the people's homes or the schools and that can encourage a positive response if people want to donate to a charity to help these people. On the other hand, there are newspapers that sensationalise news also and show unnecessary pictures of like maybe a car accident, a victim of that. Nobody needs to see that sort of blood or gore. Nobody needs to see that. So some pictures are not appropriate but some are.

OK, thank you. That is the end of the speaking test.

Sample 8
Gifts and Culture
礼物与文化

Part 1 *MP3 21*

Hello, my name is (examiner's name).
What's your full name please?
Can I check your ID and passport please?
In the first part, I'd like to ask you some general questions about yourself.

Let's talk about where you live.
- What do you like about the place you live in?
- How can you make the place you live in better?
- Would you consider moving to a new place?

Now I'd like to talk about shopping.
- Do you often go shopping?
- Do you prefer to go shopping alone or with friends?
- What do you like to buy when you go shopping?

Let's discuss age.
- Is it polite to ask someone's age in your culture?
- What can you do to keep looking young?
- When is the best age to get married?

Part 2

In Part 2, I will give you a topic and I'd like you to talk about it for 1-2 minutes. Before you talk, you will have one minute to think about what you are going to say. You may make some notes if you wish. Do you understand?

Topic Card

Describe a gift that you have given to someone. You should say: ■ what it was ■ who you gave it to ■ why you bought/made it and explain how you and the person who received it felt?

■ Do you often give presents?
■ Do you prefer to give or receive presents?

Part 3

You've been talking about a gift that you have given to someone and I'd like to ask you one or two more general questions related to this.
Let's consider first of all:

Gifts and culture
■ Identify the times when you give gifts in your culture.
■ Assess the importance of gift giving in your culture.
■ Compare the types of gifts people gave in the past to those given nowadays in your culture.

Homemade gifts
■ Consider why some people like to make gifts as opposed to buying gifts.
■ Agree/Disagree that homemade gifts are more meaningful than buying presents.
■ Discuss the difficulties of making gifts on your own.

Thank you. That is the end of the speaking test.

Sample Answer 9分口语范例

SCRIPT 对话内容

The following script is of native speakers. 以下对话中的考生是母语为英语的外国人。

Part 1

Hello, my name is Jonathon McGovern. What's your full name please?

My name is Ryan Lockhart.

Can I check your ID and passport please?

Sure. Here you go.

Very good. In the first part, I'd like to ask you some general questions about yourself. Let's talk about where you live. What do you like about the place you live in?

The thing I like about the place I live in at the moment is that we're on the top floor which means we get lots of natural lighting. Often especially when you're living, I'm living in Taipei, so when you're living in Taipei there are many different high-rise buildings and so you don't get a lot of natural lighting but with my place, good, lots of natural light.

How can you make the place you live in better?

There are many ways that I could make it better. I suppose, I'm a big fan of "bigger is better" so at the moment it's not that big. There are 3 bedrooms; however, I would like to have a balcony. If we could have a balcony, that would be really good.

Would you consider moving to a new place?

Sure. I often move to new places. I'm very used to moving around the place, moving to different cities, moving to different countries. So if there is a bigger and better place with my balcony, then I would move.

Now I'd like to talk about shopping. Do you often go shopping?

I do go shopping. It's probably not often. Generally when I go shopping, I don't go shopping for myself. I usually buy presents or gifts for other people.

Do you prefer to go shopping alone or with friends?

I definitely, 100%, prefer to go shopping alone. I like to be in and out because actually I don't like shopping. Alright and if I am with somebody else and they're looking at different things and saying: "Is this ok? Do you like this one? Do you want this one?" I get really frustrated. I got this, this all started back when I was a child and I had to go shopping with my mother and my older sister. It was always a nightmare.

What do you like to buy when you go shopping?

If I go shopping for myself, I probably prefer to buy, I like to buy clothes though I haven't done that for a long time. I also like to buy electronic goods so you know things like iPods and, or a PSP, or you know all those computer games, that kind of stuff. Maybe phones, I love phones.

Good. Let's discuss age. Is it polite to ask someone's age in your culture?

Generally speaking it isn't. I mean, especially if you're talking to a female, you should never ask a female how old she is. She might get very upset. Males sometimes, I mean you can get away with it but generally speaking you shouldn't ask someone's age unless you're good friends of course.

What can you do to keep looking young?

Well, obviously if you wanna keep looking young, I think for guys probably you should do lots of sports and exercise. Make sure that you're fit and healthy and that generally makes you look younger. For women, they can take lots of short cuts. They can use things like make-up to hide wrinkles and they put lots of cream on, exfoliates and things like that, I think they are called. So they've got lots of other things at their disposal to make them look young.

When is the best age to get married?

Well, it really depends on the person. I don't think there's actually an ideal age for when you should get married. Some believe you should get married young because then, for example if you have kids, they grow up more quickly and then when you're maybe only 40 or 50 years old, they've already grown up. They're getting a job and then you still have a lot of freedom to go and travel the world. Whereas others prefer to get married when they're a little bit older. That way they can save more money and then when they do have kids, they are able to offer them you know a better education, a better standard of living in general.

Part 2

In Part 2, I will give you a topic and I'd like you to talk about it for one to two minutes. Before you talk, you will have one minute to think about what you are going to say. You may make some notes if you wish. Do you understand?

Sure.

Right. Here's your pen and paper. Here's your topic card. Could you describe a gift that you have given to someone?

I often give gifts. Actually, I like giving gifts. I like giving gifts more than receiving gifts. The person that I probably buy the most gifts for is my mother. So it doesn't matter if it's Mother's Day or if it's Christmas or it's her birthday, I always make a big deal out of buying a gift that I think that she'll enjoy. So for example for last Mother's Day, I was thinking about what I can buy for her and I remembered when I was much younger, when I was still probably maybe in primary school or high school, I always told my mum "when I get older mum and I get lots of money and I am rich, I'm going to buy you a Porsche, alright". However now that I'm older, I'm still not rich. I can't buy her a Porsche but I thought I could do the next best thing so I rented a Porsche for her for the day. So what happened was the Porsche got delivered to her doorstep and I told a big lie and said "that was for you mum. I just bought this Porsche." And at the end of the day, I had to tell her the truth and said "you have to give it back now." But she got to drive around the Porsche for the day and it also included a picnic basket in the back. So she went with my stepfather, her husband and they drove off somewhere. I don't know where they drove off to coz I didn't get to go unfortunately and then they had the picnic lunch and then they came back and she had a great day. So generally speaking I like to buy gifts that are an experience so it's not just like an object that you give to someone and they say "oh that's great!" I like to make it an experience. Something they can enjoy for maybe one hour, two hours or one full day.

Do you often give presents?

Actually probably not that often. I mean if it's someone special like my wife or my girlfriend, then I will give a present but I don't give presents just to anybody.

<u>Part 3</u>

Right. You've been talking about giving gifts. I'd like to ask you one or two more questions related to this. Let's first talk about gifts and culture. Identify the times when you give gifts in your culture.

OK, in Australia, we give gifts definitely for Christmas especially if there's, if you have young children or if you know some young children. Obviously this is probably the happiest time for kids because they get presents from lots and lots of different people. Apart from Christmas we also give it for birthdays. Again, it's very important again for kids but we still do it for adults also and then there's other times like Valentine's Day. Actually I think the whole gift giving thing has become quite commercial so shopping centres have clued onto the fact that "hey it's a festival, people have to give gifts." And they try to push us and you know make us want to give more and more gifts on all these different occasions like Valentine's Day, Christmas, etc. even Easter.

Assess the importance of gift giving in your culture.

I think it is quite important. Obviously if it's your, like your mother's or your girlfriend's or your boyfriend's birthday and you don't give them a gift, then

I'm sure they are going to be quite upset alright. At least you have to make some kind of acknowledgement that today it's your birthday. You know have a happy birthday but it's expected I think by most people "hey it's your birthday, you should receive a gift from your loved ones."

Compare the types of gifts people gave in the past to those given nowadays in your culture.

In the past, obviously there weren't as many different types of gifts so they were usually some kind of material object that you would give them. You probably, I think in the past probably people made homemade gifts more also whereas these days there are so many products available in shops and on the market that you can buy absolutely anything. I mean there are even silly things you can buy these days and then nowadays also you have so many more technological products that you can buy which you didn't have in the past so you didn't have things like iPods or iPhones in the past which you do have now. So these are also quite a popular present to give.

Let's now talk about homemade gifts. Consider why some people like to make gifts as opposed to buying gifts.

I think people like to make gifts because they feel it's much more meaningful. It's much more personal. It's something that comes from the heart because obviously it's much easier just to go into any old shop and say "OK that looks like a decent present for my friend or for my parents. I'll just buy that right?" Which is quite easy to do. Whereas as soon as somebody receives a homemade gift they say "huh, that's wonderful." You know you've spent so much time on this. You know it shows how much you value this friendship or how much you value this relationship. And I think that's the main reason why people like to make homemade gifts.

Do you agree or disagree that homemade gifts are more meaningful than buying presents?

Not necessarily. Obviously it's easy to buy a present but when you're buying a present you can also put a lot of thought into the type of present that you buy so you don't just go out and buy the first thing that you see.

You think about now why am I buying this. You know does it have any meaning like has anything happened in the past where they will say "Oh I'm so happy you bought me this! How did you know?" So buying presents can also be meaningful as long as you think about why you're getting this present for that person.

Discuss the difficulties of making gifts on your own.

Well obviously if you're not very creative, that's going to be one obstacle because when you're making your own gift, you need to be imaginative, creative. Another problem might be if you're making things you might have to have some kind of artistic talent or some kind of, you know you have to be good with handicrafts so you can make these things, not everybody has this type of skill, not everybody has this type of talent, so for example maybe you wanted to make a card alright? And then the card obviously you want to make the card pretty. You don't just want it to be a plain piece of white paper so you need to have some ideas on how, you need to be good at maybe drawing or you need to be good at for example putting some kind of tinsel or some kind of other objects on it. You can tell that I'm not that artistic and good at making homemade gifts. I'm the type of person that probably prefers to buy a gift.

Thank you. That is the end of the speaking test.

IELTS

SUPERIOR SPEAKING

主题分类问题集

Topic-Based Question Bank

Topic-Based Question Bank

The following section contains a large topic-based question bank. Use these questions as practice with yourself or your study partners. The following topics are some of the most frequently encountered in the official test. Make sure you understand what all the questions are asking you to do. You can also listen to the recordings and provide answers as you hear them.

此篇收录以主题分类的“问题集”，这些主题在 IELTS 考试中经常出现。此部分有录音，你可以试着自己或找朋友一起练习这些题目，并确定自己能了解问题的重点。

Hometowns · Cities · Countries

家乡·城市·国家

MP3 22

Part 1
口试 Part 1

Hometown 家乡

- Where's your hometown?
- Where do you live now?
- Is there anything you don't like about your hometown?
- Is your hometown big or small?
- Does anyone famous come from your hometown?
- Could you describe the landscape of your hometown?
- What is some of the history of your hometown?
- When is the best time to visit your hometown?
- What's the best thing about your hometown?
- How do you think your hometown will change in the future?
- How long have you lived in your hometown?
- Do you like your hometown?
- Would you rather live in your hometown or another city?
- What's the difference between your hometown and other cities in your country?

Neighbourhood 邻近地区

- What is the area like where you live?
- What's your neighbourhood like?
- What kinds of jobs do people have in your neighbourhood?
- Do you get along with your neighbours?
- Is your home in a convenient location?
- Is your neighbourhood a safe place to live?

Cities 城市

- What is your city famous for?
- What should a tourist do if they visit your city?
- What would you like to change about your city?
- How can you make your city better?
- What are the main industries in your city?

- What kinds of amenities does your city offer?
- Is it easy to get around your city?
- How has your city developed over the past few decades?
- Could you describe the layout of your city?
- Why do people move to the city?

Countries 国家

- Describe the geography of your country.
- What are some social issues your country has?
- What are some global issues?
- What can you do to make the world a better place to live?
- What's the standard of living like in your country?

Lifestyle 生活方式

- How can you improve your quality of life?
- What are the advantages of living in the country?
- Where would you like to live when you retire?

Part 2
口试 Part 2

Describe **where you would like to retire**.
You should say:
- where it is
- what it's like
- why you like this place

and explain how this place makes you feel.

Describe **a problem in your city**.
You should say:
- what it is
- how it was caused
- why it is a problem

and offer some solutions to the problem.

Describe **a famous place in your country**.
You should say:
- where it is
- what it's famous for
- who visits the place

and explain *how/why* it became famous.

Describe **a place you often went to as a child**.
You should say:
- where it was
- who you went there with
- what you did there

and explain why you often went there.

Part 3
口试 Part 3

Living Standards 生活水准

- Is the government doing enough to raise the standard of living?
- How does a city shape who you are or become?
- Which is more important, raising the standard of living or protecting the environment?
- What factors determine a country's standard of living?

Globalisation 全球化

- What role does the UN play?
- Do you think the world is becoming smaller?
- What are the major differences between your country and other nations?
- What can you learn from other countries and cultures?

Growth of Cities 城市发展

- How have cities in your country developed since your parents were young?
- What will cities be like in the future?
- What is the cause of urbanisation?

- What is the downside of urbanisation?
- How is overpopulation caused?

Society 社会

- Are people isolating themselves from society these days?
- What responsibilities do citizens of a nation have?
- How does unemployment affect society?

Immigration 移民

- Why do people emigrate?
- What kind of problems may immigrants experience when they arrive in a new country?
- Does immigration threaten local culture or enhance it?
- What can be done about illegal immigration?
- Does immigration have a positive or negative effect on the economy?

Developing Countries 发展中国家

- What can the government do to ensure the equal distribution of wealth?
- What can we do to assist developing countries?
- What are the causes of poverty in a nation?

Work
工作

MP3 23

Part 1
口试 Part 1

Your Job 你的工作

- Do you work or are you a student?
- What do you like about your job?
- What don't you enjoy about your work?
- How do you travel to work?
- When would you like to retire?
- Describe a typical day in your job.
- What do you find most difficult about your job?
- What other jobs would you be interested in?
- Which job wouldn't you like to do?
- Would you like a job in which you could travel? *Why/Why not*?
- What training do you need for your job?

Companies 公司

- Is your company a good one? *Why/Why not*?
- Would you like to run your own business? *Why/Why not*?
- What is the ideal work environment?

Employers 雇主

- Do you like your boss? *Why/Why not*?
- What's the best way to prepare for a job interview?
- Do you prefer male or female bosses?

Employees 职员

- Do women usually work after they get married in your country?
- Is it easy to find a job in your country?

Part 2
口试 Part 2

Describe **a successful company you know**.
You should say:
- what it is
- what you know about the company
- why you liked this company

and explain how it became successful.

Describe **the kind of boss you like**.
You should say:
- what they teach you
- what qualifications they need
- what qualities they need

and explain why they would be a good boss.

Describe **what makes a good employee**.
You should say:
- what qualifications they need
- what qualities they need
- what attitude they should have

and explain why it's important to be a good employee.

Describe **a memorable day you had at work**.
You should say:
- when it was
- who was there
- what made it memorable

and explain how you felt that day.

Part 3
口试 Part 3

Workforce 人力资源
- What are the characteristics of a good employee? And employer?
- What are the benefits and shortcomings of being a manager?
- How important is teamwork?

Unemployment 失业

- What problems does unemployment cause?
- What can be done about the problems that unemployment causes?
- Why is it difficult to find a good job?

Work Conditions 工作环境

- Which is more important, a good salary or a job you enjoy?
- Why do many people become workaholics?
- What factors influence job choice?
- How important is job interest?
- What are the perfect work conditions?
- How serious is the problem of unfair labour practices?
- How could the government improve employment conditions in your country?

Work Discrimination 工作歧视

- Which jobs are considered prestigious in your country and why?
- Is work discrimination a problem in your country?
- How are female bosses different from male bosses?
- Do men's jobs differ from women's in your country?

The Development of Jobs 职业发展

- How have jobs changed over the past 50 years in your country?
- How will jobs change in the future?
- Do you think young people are becoming less and less hard-working?

Work and Education 工作与教育

- Which is more important, educational qualifications or work experience?
- Does the education system in your country adequately prepare people for the workforce?
- Do employers prefer degrees from foreign universities or local ones in your country?

Education
教育

MP3 24

Part 1
口试 Part 1

Studies 学业
- Do you work or are you a student?
- What do you like about your studies?
- Which subjects don't you enjoy?
- What don't you enjoy about your studies?
- What's the best way to prepare for a test?

School 学校
- Is your school a good one? *Why/Why not*?
- What facilities does your school have?
- What are teachers like in your country?
- Are your school tuition fees expensive?
- Do you like school uniforms?
- How do you travel to school?
- Do you belong to any school clubs?
- How strict is your school?

English 英文
- Why are you studying English?
- Why do you need IELTS?
- What do you find most difficult about learning a language?
- What is your strength in English?
- Did you learn a foreign language at primary or high school?

Part 2
口试 Part 2

Describe **a teacher who has influenced you**.
You should say:
- who *he/she* was
- what they taught you
- why you liked this teacher

and explain how they influenced you.

Describe **something you have learnt that is very useful.**
You should say:
- what it is
- how you learnt it
- who taught you

and explain why it is so useful.

Describe **something that you would love to learn.**
You should say:
- what it is
- how you will learn it
- what it may lead to in the future

and explain why you are interested in it.

Describe **a memorable day you had at school.**
You should say:
- when it was
- who was there
- what made it memorable

and explain how you felt that day.

Part 3
口试 Part 3

Primary & Secondary Education 小学及中学教育

- Do you think it's better to learn in a coeducational or single sex school?
- Could you compare public schools to state schools?
- Do you think you learn more from your teachers or your parents?
- What's the best way to punish students if they have broken a school rule?
- What are the advantages and disadvantages of school uniforms?
- Would you agree that exams are the best way to measure what a student has learnt?

Tertiary Education 专科 / 大学教育

- Which factors determine which university to attend?
- How important is a tertiary education in getting a job in your country?
- What do you think of the saying "Experience is the best teacher"?

Ministry of Education 教育部

- Should education be free?
- Do women have the same education opportunities in your country as men?
- How serious is the problem of illiteracy in your country?
- How can highly experienced and qualified teachers be encouraged to teach in rural areas?
- How could the government improve the education system in your country?

Development of Education 教育发展

- Which subjects at school are becoming increasingly important?
- How has education changed over the past 50 years in your country?
- How will education change in the future?

Crime
犯罪

MP3 25

Part 1
口试 Part 1

Public Safety 公共安全

- Is your hometown a safe city?
- Are there any parts of your city that are too dangerous to visit?
- Is it safe to walk outside alone at night?
- Do you always lock your house and car?

Crimes 犯罪

- What are some common crimes committed in your country?
- Do you ever drink and drive?
- Are there any problems with drugs where you live?
- What crimes have you heard about in the news recently?
- What are prisons like in your country?
- Have you ever seen a crime?
- What would you do if you heard a burglar in your home?
- Have you ever been the victim of a crime?

Part 2
口试 Part 2

Describe **a school rule that you don't like or disagree with.**
You should say:
- what it is
- why the rule exists
- why you don't like the rule

and offer some alternatives to the rule.

Describe **what crimes affect the area you live in.**
You should say:
- what they are
- how they affect people
- how often they occur

and explain why they happen.

Describe **what makes a good police officer**.
You should say:
- what qualifications and training they need
- what qualities they need
- what responsibilities they have

and explain why it's important to be a good police officer.

Describe **a crime that you have heard about**.
You should say:
- when it was
- who was there
- what happened

and explain how you feel about the crime.

Part 3
口试 Part 3

Development of Crime 犯罪的发展

- How have crimes changed over the last 50 years in your country?
- How will crimes change in the future?
- Could you compare blue- to white-collar crime?
- Do you think abortion is a crime?
- How concerned are you about terrorism?
- Are you optimistic that in the future we will be living in a safer society?

Deterring Crime 遏制犯罪

- Do you believe public executions would deter crime?
- How important is education in preventing crime?
- Do you think gun control is a good idea?
- Do you think police should be allowed to carry guns?
- Do you think the punishment for violent crimes should be the same for juveniles?

Criminal Behaviour 犯罪行为

- Why do people become criminals?
- Is it possible to change a criminal into a law-abiding citizen?
- Do you think there is link between drugs and crime?
- What are the characteristics of gangs in your country?

Security Forces 保安

- How could the government improve public safety in your country?
- What rights should criminals have while in jail?
- How effective are the police in your country in preventing crime?
- How tough is your government on organised crime?

Entertainment
娱乐

MP3 26

Part 1
口试 Part 1

Music 音乐
- What kind of music do you like?
- Do you prefer western music or Chinese music?
- Can you play a musical instrument?

TV & Movies 电视与电影
- Where's the best movie theatre in your *town/city*?
- Why are movies popular?
- What is the difference between watching a movie at home and at the theatre?
- How much TV do people watch?
- What kind of programmes do you enjoy watching on TV?
- Can TV help you learn English?

Going Out 出去玩
- What do you think of gambling?
- What can you do in the evenings?
- Do you enjoy dancing?
- Have you ever tried Karaoke?
- Do you have any amusement parks?
- What's the best museum or art gallery?
- Which form of entertainment do you enjoy the most?

Literature 文学
- Where do you like to read?
- What genre of books don't you like?
- Do you ever read English books or magazines?

Stars 明星
- Which star would you like to meet?
- Who's a famous *actor/singer* from your country?
- What kind of star would you like to be?

Part 2
口试 Part 2

Describe **a book you read as a child.**
You should say:
■ what book it was
■ what it was about
■ why you liked it
and explain what you've learnt from it.

Describe **the last movie you saw.**
You should say:
■ what movie it was
■ what it was about
■ what was special about it
and explain why you enjoyed it.

Describe **someone famous that you admire.**
You should say:
■ who it is
■ what they do
■ how they became successful
and explain why you admire them.

Describe **your favourite place to go for entertainment.**
You should say:
■ what and where it is
■ what you can do there
■ what the atmosphere is like
and explain why you enjoy it there.

Part 3
口试 Part 3

Development of Entertainment 休闲娱乐发展

- How has entertainment changed over the past 50 years?
- How will entertainment change in the future?
- What's the difference between reading a book and watching the movie?

Entertainment and Education 娱乐与教育

- Do you think TV is educational?
- How can parents ensure that children only watch suitable material on TV?
- What can you learn from museums?

Fame and Success 名望与成就

- Do you think movie stars and actors earn too much money?
- How much influence do celebrities have on youngsters?
- What are the disadvantages of fame and success?
- Which is most important to you, fame, success or wealth?
- Why are we so interested in the private lives of celebrities?
- What responsibilities do famous people have to society and children in particular?

Entertainment Issues 休闲娱乐话题

- Should movies be censored?
- What effect, if any, does violence on TV and movies have on children?
- What problems may compulsive gamblers encounter?
- How serious is the problem of pirated movies in your country?
- What effect does downloading mp3s illegally have on the artist?

Environment

环境

MP3 27

Part 1
口试 Part 1

Recycling 资源回收

- What can you recycle?
- How is garbage collected in your neighbourhood?
- Do you waste energy?

Clean Environment 干净的环境

- What types of pollution are there in your city?
- Do you often take public transport?
- Are you educated about protecting the environment at school?
- What do you do to protect the environment?

Wildlife 野生动物

- What animals can you see in the wild in your country?
- Are you afraid of bugs?
- Do you like watching animals in the wild?

Nature 大自然

- How often do you enjoy nature?
- What are some places tourists can visit to enjoy nature in your country?
- Does your country often suffer from natural disasters? Which one(s)?
- What do you do if there is a typhoon or earthquake?

Part 2
口试 Part 2

Describe **an environmental issue in your city**.
You should say:
- what it is
- how it is caused
- what it results in

and offer some solutions to the problem.

Describe **a natural disaster that has occurred in your country**.
You should say:
- what it was
- when it was
- what destruction it caused

and explain how it made you feel.

Describe **a place of natural beauty in your country**.
You should say:
- where it is
- what you can do there
- when the best time to go is

and explain what makes it so attractive.

Describe **a type of public transport in your city**.
You should say:
- what it is
- what the advantages are
- what the disadvantages are

and offer some alternatives to this form of public transport.

Part 3
口试 Part 3

Environmental Destruction 环境破坏
- What are the environmental effects of urbanisation?
- What are the main causes of pollution in your area?
- How concerned are you about the environment?
- How noticeable is the problem of deforestation in your country?

Environmental Protection 环境保护
- What effect would banning cars from city centres have?
- What can we do to make this world a better place?
- What can we learn from nature?

Environmental Changes 环境变化

- How has the environment changed since you were a child?
- Are you optimistic about the future of our environment?
- How can we strike a balance between development and protection?

Alternative Energies 替代能源

- What are some alternative energy sources that can be developed more?
- What are the pros and cons of alternative energy such as solar power?
- What dangers are there in the production of nuclear power?

Environment and the Government 环境与政府

- Should the government make the environment a priority?
- Is the government doing enough to protect the environment?
- Which is more important, increasing the standard of living or protecting the environment?
- Who is more responsible for protecting the environment, individuals or governments?
- Are governments tough enough on companies which break environmental laws?

Endangered Species 濒临绝种生物

- Are there any endangered species in your country?
- Do you agree that all animals should be protected?
- What causes the extinction of some species?

Media
媒体

MP3 28

Part 1
口试 Part 1

News 新闻
- Which are you more interested in, local or international news?
- What don't you like about the news?
- Why are people interested in the news?
- Should you always keep up with the latest news?

TV, Radio & Internet News 电视、广播及网络新闻
- Where do you get your news from? TV? Radio? Internet?
- Can you understand the English news on TV?
- What's the difference between news from the radio and that from TV?

Newspapers 报纸
- What sections of a newspaper do you prefer?
- When and where do you read newspapers?
- How can newspapers help you improve your English?

Part 2
口试 Part 2

Describe **a newspaper you enjoy reading**.
You should say:
- what the newspaper is
- what sections it has
- when and how often you read it

and explain why you like it.

Describe **a recent news event**.
You should say:
- what it was
- when it happened
- where it happened

and explain how you felt when you heard about it.

Describe **a radio station you like listening to.**
You should say:
- what it is called
- what kind of music they play
- what kind of programmes they have

and explain why you like it.

Describe **a TV or radio ad you like.**
You should say:
- what the product is
- how it is promoted
- what makes it different from other ads

and explain why you like it.

Part 3
口试 Part 3

Role & Influence of Media 媒体的角色及影响力

- What role does the media play?
- How can the media influence young people?
- To what extent should we trust the media?
- What news must people know about? What do they not need to know?

Development of Media 媒体发展

- How has the media developed over the past 50 years?
- How are newspapers different these days compared to the past?
- How has the media contributed to globalisation?

Media Issues 媒体话题

- Should the media be censored?
- Why does the media sensationalise the news?
- Is the news too shocking now?
- Is there too much advertising on the TV and radio?
- Why does the media often come under scrutiny for stories they publish?
- Do you think tabloids should be banned?

3C (Computers, Cameras & Communications)

3C 产品

MP3 29

Part 1
口试 Part 1

Computers 电脑

- When did you learn to use a computer?
- How did you learn to use a computer?
- What do you use a computer for?
- How well can you type?
- Do you ever play computer games?
- Are computers expensive in your country?
- Have you ever used a computer to improve your English?

Cameras 相机

- Do you have a camera? What kind?
- When and why do you take photos?
- Are digital cameras better than cameras with film?
- Do you prefer to take photos of people, places or things?

Communications 通讯

- Why are mobile phones so popular?
- What other forms of communication do you use?
- How good are you at sending text messages in English?
- What does your mobile phone look like?
- Do you prefer sending a text message or talking on your mobile?

Internet 网络

- What do you use the Internet for?
- Have you ever bought anything from the Internet?
- Do you like to chat on the Internet?
- Do you think you spend too much time on the net?
- Do you have a favourite website?
- Do you ever write English emails?
- Do you still write letters? Why or why not?

Part 2
口试 Part 2

Describe **a website you find interesting or useful**.
You should say:
- what it is
- how you found it
- what information it provides
and explain why you like it.

Describe **a communication tool you use**.
You should say:
- what it is
- what functions it has
- why you use it
and explain what makes it useful.

Describe **a memorable photo you have**.
You should say:
- when and where it was taken
- what you were doing at the time
- how often you look at it
and explain what makes it so memorable.

Describe **an electronic device you would like to learn more about**.
You should say:
- what it is
- what functions it has
- how you will learn to use it
and explain why it would be useful to learn.

Part 3
口试 Part 3

Development of Technology 科技发展

- How will the Internet develop in the future?
- How have computers changed our lives?
- What effect have mobile phones had on our lives?

Technology and Children 科技与儿童

- How important is it that each child has access to a computer?
- Could you explain why the Internet is unsafe for young kids?
- What responsibilities do parents have to protect their children from the dangers of the Internet?
- How could the Internet be made safer?
- Do you think children need mobile phones?
- How serious is the problem of phone abuse in school time by students?

Technology and Society 科技与社会

- How has technology aided education and learning?
- What right does the government have to censor the Internet?
- What are the benefits of mobile phones?
- What are the advantages and disadvantages of email?

Sports · Recreation
运动·休闲

MP3 30

Part 1
口试 Part 1

Sports 体育运动
- What sports are you good at?
- What sports is your country famous for?
- What sporting or exercise facilities do you have in your community?
- Have you ever been the member of a sports team?
- Do you prefer to watch sporting events live or on TV?
- Do you prefer team or individual sports?
- What's the most dangerous sport you've played?
- Who is a famous sports person from your country?
- Which sport do you not like to watch or play?

Exercise 健身
- What do you do to keep fit?
- What are the dangers of swimming at the beach?
- How often do you exercise or play sport?

Leisure 闲暇时光
- What leisure activities do you enjoy?
- Do you have enough leisure time?
- Is it easy to find places to relax in your neighbourhood?

Part 2
口试 Part 2

Describe **a leisure activity that you enjoy**.
You should say:
- what it is
- what equipment you need
- where you do it

and explain why you enjoy it.

Describe **a relaxing activity**.
You should say:
- what it is
- where you do it
- how it relaxes you

and explain why you enjoy it.

Describe **a dangerous sport**.
You should say:
- what it is
- where you can do it
- who takes part in it

and explain why it is dangerous.

Describe **a famous sportsperson you know**.
You should say:
- who the person is
- what they play
- where they play

and explain how or why they became successful.

Part 3
口试 Part 3

Sporting Success 运动带来的成功

- Would you agree that sports stars earn too much money?
- What are the effects of parents who become too involved in their children's sports activities?
- What responsibilities do sports stars have to society?

Sports Issues 运动话题

- Has sport become too commercialised these days?
- Do you think world sporting events, like the Olympics, promote international understanding?
- Do you think gambling on sporting events is acceptable?
- What should be the punishment for sports people who take performance-enhancing drugs?

Healthy Nation 健康的国家

- What does your government do to encourage people to lead a healthy lifestyle?
- How do you think sports and exercise may develop in the future?
- What are the benefits of having sports as part of the school curriculum?

Food · Dining
饮食

MP3 31

Part 1
口试 Part 1

Food 食物

- What can you cook?
- What's the strangest food you have ever eaten?
- What food can't you stand?
- How often do you eat dinner with your family?
- What kinds of desserts are popular in your country?
- What kinds of fruit and vegetables are grown in your country?
- Who does the grocery shopping in your home?
- What food from your country would you miss the most if you were living abroad?
- What food from you country would you suggest a foreigner try?

Restaurants 餐厅

- Do you prefer to eat at a restaurant or at home?
- How often do you eat at fast food restaurants?
- Is it customary to tip at restaurants in your country?
- Who usually pays for the meal when going out to eat in your country?

Diet 饮食

- What do you think of health food?
- Do you like food from other countries?
- Do you eat food now that you didn't eat as a child?
- Is vegetarianism popular in your country?
- Do you eat regular meals?
- How concerned are you about your health and diet?
- Do you often eat snacks between meals?
- Have you ever had food poisoning?

Part 2
口试 Part 2

Describe **your favourite health food**.
You should say:
- what it is
- when and how often you eat it
- how and where it is made

and explain why it is healthy.

Describe **some traditional food from your country**.
You should say:
- what it is
- when and how often you eat it
- how and where it is made

and explain what it tastes like.

Describe **a restaurant you like**.
You should say:
- what kind of food it has
- what kind of atmosphere it has
- where it is

and explain what makes it special.

Part 3
口试 Part 3

Health Issues 健康话题

- Is child obesity a problem in your country?
- Do diets work or are they just a quick way for some business-minded people to make money?
- What are the effects of an unhealthy diet?
- What can the government do to encourage a healthy lifestyle among its citizens?

Dietary Changes 饮食习惯的改变

- How have eating habits changed over the past 50 years?
- What explanations can you provide for the growing popularity of organic food?
- What are the pros and cons of being vegetarian?
- Would you agree that people eat more healthily than in the past?
- How important is it to you to have a balanced diet?

Food and Culture 饮食与文化

- What are the main differences between Asian and Western food?
- What significance does food have in your culture?
- Do some cultures have a healthier diet than others?

Health · Medicine
健康·医药

MP3 32

Part 1
口试 Part 1

Medical Centres & Practitioners 医疗中心与执业者

- How often do you have a health check-up?
- Are gyms and health spas popular in your country?
- Are you afraid of dentists?
- Have you ever tried traditional Chinese medicine?
- Do you prefer western or natural medicine?

Relaxation 放松，消遣

- How do you deal with stress?
- How do you relax after work or studies?
- Where is the best place to go to relax in your *town/city*?
- Do you have enough relaxation time?

Illnesses 疾病

- What do you usually do when you catch a cold?
- What do you do to stay healthy?
- Do you suffer from an allergy?
- Have you ever broken a bone?
- Who looks after you when you are sick?
- Do you often take days off sick from work or studies?
- What is a traditional remedy for a cold in your culture?

Part 2
口试 Part 2

Describe **an unhealthy habit you have**.
You should say:
- what it is
- when and how often you do it
- why it is unhealthy

and explain what you can do about it.

Describe **an illness you have had**.
You should say:
- what it was
- when and how long you had it
- how you got it and how you felt

and explain what you did about it.

Describe **a time when you or someone you know were injured**.
You should say:
- how the injury occurred
- what treatment was taken
- how the lifestyle of you or the person you know was affected

and explain how you or the person you know felt during the time.

Describe **a doctor you know or have visited**.
You should say:
- who *he/she* is
- what kind of medicine *he/she* practises
- how effective *he/she* is

and explain when and how you met.

Part 3
口试 Part 3

Healthcare 医疗护理
- How effective is the healthcare system in your country?
- Do you think people will become more or less healthy in the future?
- What are the benefits and drawbacks of not seeing a doctor when you are sick?
- Could you compare the healthcare facilities in rural and urban areas?
- What dangers are there of taking medicine?

Health Authorities 公共卫生机关

- What can the government do to improve health conditions for the elderly?
- What responsibilities do doctors have?
- What is the role of the government in healthcare?
- Do you agree that doctors are underpaid?

Health Issues 健康话题

- Why do people smoke?
- What are the effects of smoking?
- How concerned are you about the spread of diseases?

Travel · Transportation · Holidays · Culture
旅游·交通工具·假期·文化

MP3 33

Part 1
口试 Part 1

Travel 旅游

- Which countries have you been to?
- How often do you travel abroad or intercity?
- Do you prefer to travel alone or in a group?
- Do you prefer package tours or independent travel?
- What country do you want to visit most? Why?
- What kind of accommodation do you prefer to stay in while travelling?
- What are the benefits of travel?
- Can travel be dangerous?
- Would you travel back to a place you have been to before and stay there again?

Transportation 交通工具

- Do you have a driver's licence?
- Do you prefer to travel by bus, train, ship, plane or car?
- Do you have a good sense of direction?
- What is the most popular form of public transportation in your *town/city*?
- How often do you take public transportation?
- Do you ever ride a bike these days?
- How do you travel to work or school?
- Is it easy to find a parking space in your *town/city*?
- What mode of transportation do you think is the safest?

Holidays 假期

- Do you prefer summer or winter holidays?
- Do you prefer active or relaxing holidays?
- What holidays are celebrated as a family in your culture?
- What foods are eaten for your favourite holiday?
- Would you like more holidays?

Culture 文化

- What is *interesting/special* about your culture?
- What don't you like about your culture?
- Are you familiar with any other cultures? Which ones?
- Which culture would you most like to learn more about?
- Do you practise any traditional customs?

Part 2
口试 Part 2

Describe **your ideal holiday**.
You should say:
- where you would go
- when and how long you would go for
- who you would go with

and explain what would be special about this holiday.

Describe **a car you would like to buy**.
You should say:
- what it is
- what features it would have
- how it compares to other cars

and explain why you would like to buy it.

Describe **a place you would like to go for a company or school trip**.
You should say:
- where you would like to go
- what you could do there
- when and how long you would go for

and explain why it would suit the other members of the group.

Describe **an aspect of your culture that you are most proud of**.
You should say:
- what it is
- what makes it special
- how it originated

and explain why you are proud of it.

Part 3
口试 Part 3

Transportation Issues 交通运输话题
- How effective is the public transportation system in your *town/city*?
- What could the government do to improve the public transportation system in your *town/city*?
- What is the cause of traffic congestion?
- What does traffic congestion lead to?

Tourism Industry 观光事业
- How concerned are you about air travel?
- What responsibilities do tourists have when visiting a foreign country?
- What are the pros and cons of tourism?
- Could you compare the benefits of international travel to domestic?

Development of Tourism 观光业的发展
- How can the government attract more tourists to your country?
- How has the tourism industry changed over the past 50 years?
- How may it develop in the future?

Cultural Identity 文化认同

- Which customs are dying out in your country?
- How has globalisation affected your culture?
- How much respect does the younger generation in your country have towards your culture and customs?
- Do you think that many public holidays are losing their significance nowadays?

Topic-Based Glossary

The following vocabulary if used correctly would typify some of the vocabulary an IELTS 7 and above candidate would produce. It has been arranged according to topic and includes a number of idioms.

以下的词汇及惯用语若能融会贯通，那么你的程度就可以说已达到了 IELTS 考试 7 分或以上的程度了。若不懂其用法，可参照页码(即单词后面括号中的数字)回内文找出处，并熟记用法。

Actions/Activities	
■ at one's disposal (152) ■ compose scores for (156) ■ fumbling (149) ■ go clubbing (135) ■ hive of activity (67) ■ intense (164) ■ jingle for (156) ■ make sth into a fine art (109)	■ recede (136) ■ settle (43) ■ short of sth to do (68) ■ sift through (83) ■ spoil oneself with sth (78) ■ stimulate (137) ■ sweat profusely (150)

Appearance	
■ aesthetic (164) ■ athletic (179) ■ be aesthetically pleasing (124) ■ be nothing short of spectacular (68) ■ drab (5)	■ dwarf (73) ■ philanthropist (174) ■ photogenic (181) ■ picturesque (67) ■ tarnish (9)

Crime/War	
■ abide by the law (166) ■ blue-collar crime (204) ■ bribe (166) ■ burglar (203) ■ capital punishment (165) ■ codified (159) ■ commit murder (165) ■ conquer (47)	■ death penalty (167) ■ deterrent (165) ■ eruptions of sporadic violence (8) ■ evidence (165) ■ guilty (165) ■ imprison (45) ■ just cause (166) ■ law-abiding (205)

- legislation (158)
- life imprisonment (165)
- organised crime (205)
- perpetrator (165)
- pirate (208)
- prey on sb (115)
- prison (warden) (203)
- prohibition (165)
- prove (165)
- public execution (204)
- restrain criminals (166)
- take sb into custody (166)
- terrorism (204)
- treason (165)
- trial (166)
- victim (203)
- warrior (47)
- white-collar crime (204)

Environment

- alternative energy sources (155, 211)
- chock-a-block (8)
- cold snap (9)
- deforestation (129, 210)
- earthquake (182)
- endangered species (211)
- equilibrium (9)
- extinction (211)
- flash flood (136)
- flora (159)
- hostile climate (136)
- hurricane (137)
- mudslide (182)
- nuclear power (211)
- overcast (65)
- solar power (211)
- typhoon (182)
- unharnessed (159)
- untapped resource (159)
- well-preserved (158)

Events

- bucks and hens night (112)
- colonise (8)
- get hitched (113)
- industrial revolution (8)

Feelings/Thinking

- apprehensive (170)
- be obsessed with (124)
- bored out of one's brains (68)
- carefree (95)
- compulsive (208)
- concept (159)
- daunting (iii)
- electrifying (74)
- energetic (135)
- exhilarating (158)
- figure it out (179)
- full of vitality (67)
- get sb hyped up (80)
- grateful (172)
- gruelling (180)
- inspire (164)
- malcontent (8)
- nerve-racking (iii)

- nervous breakdown (128)
- perspective (137)
- put one's nerves at ease (v)
- rewarding (156)
- spring to mind (136)
- sympathise (45)
- traumatised (137)
- vibrant (95)
- xenophobia (71)

Food

- bait (108)
- cook up a storm (61)
- organic food (147, 152, 222)
- secret family recipe (61)

Future

- forecast (175)
- get off on the right foot (iii)
- step in the right direction (iii)
- venture forth to new heights (iii)

Health

- acupuncture (150)
- allergy (223)
- cupping (150)
- easily transmitted diseases (8)
- herbal medicine (150)
- lead a balanced life (26)
- obesity (221)
- oxygen (150)
- performance-enhancing drug (218)
- reconstructive (160)
- remedy (223)
- respiration (180)
- slouch (152)
- steroid (180)
- strike a balance (211)
- treatment (224)

High Quality/Comfort

- authentic (73)
- creature comforts (159)
- extravagant (113)
- lavish (113)
- luxurious (124)
- mod con (159)
- opulent (73)
- prestigious (199)
- up-market (73)

Media

- celebrity (95)
- in the public eye (46)

- invasion of privacy (46)
- public figure (46)
- sensationalise (140, 182, 213)
- sitting in front of the box (74)
- tabloid (213)

Money/Numbers

- a hike in taxes (118)
- a large extent (137)
- be enough to live off (69)
- commercialise (218)
- declare bankruptcy (64)
- equal distribution of wealth (196)
- foot the bill (119)
- fork out (119)
- high turnover (69)
- hundreds of thousands (8)
- loads of (43)
- shoulder the cost (7)
- substantial (151)
- thousands and thousands (7)

Objects/Things

- accelerator (104)
- artefact (73)
- bouquet (113)
- brake (105)
- buoy (109)
- confetti (113)
- configuration (104)
- debris (136)
- electronic device (38, 215)
- exfoliant (160)
- function (38, 215)
- handicraft (190)
- infrastructure (8)
- ingredient (156)
- lever (104)
- loop the loop (105)
- pesticide (152)
- rod (108)
- supplement (143)
- thesaurus (149)

People

- bystander (100)
- catch up with (78)
- chauffeur (9)
- de facto relationship (113)
- diverse crowd (173)
- dubious (5)
- get in touch with (6)
- maverick (170)
- metrosexual (160)
- newlyweds (113)
- overcrowding (8)
- shape who you are (195)
- socialite (73)
- youngster (208)

Places

Popular

Problem

Social Issues

- abortion (204)
- apartheid (45)
- equality (45)
- news censorship (144)
- underage drinking (167)
- violence (145)

Solution

- clamp down (167)
- enhancement (159)
- financial aid (174)
- in search of greener pastures (69)
- introduce measures (167)
- load off one's shoulders (71)
- onus (159)
- overcome an obstacle (121)
- sth will rub off on sb (55)
- streamline (120)
- take swift measures/action (120)

Sports & Leisure

- bodysurfing (75, 157)
- boogie boarding (75)
- get a tan (75)
- sandcastle (75)
- squash (150)
- stadium (74)
- take a stroll (75)

Studies

- a wonderful lesson to learn (173)
- be well-informed (77)
- botany (159)
- coeducational (34, 201)
- corporal punishment (117)
- curriculum (133, 219)
- gain an insight (70)
- illiteracy (202)
- mantra (173)
- not know any better (105)
- single sex (201)

Success

- advent (83)
- be a big deal (104)
- be a big thing (104)
- have a natural gift for (20)
- in the right place at the right time (46)
- keep the movement going (45)
- live up to expectations (76)
- luck is on one's side (46)
- prominent (8)
- regain one's former glory (20)
- status (47)

■ stick to one's guns (45) ■ take one's turn in the spotlight (84)	■ think highly of sb/sth (70)

Task Words	
■ assess (v) ■ comment on (30) ■ define (47) ■ evaluate (10) ■ examine (8)	■ identify (60) ■ justify (38) ■ predict (4) ■ speculate (8)

Technology	
■ at the touch of a button (83) ■ computer savvy (115)	■ social networking site (179)

Time	
■ be long gone (71) ■ for hours on end (104) ■ it takes ages (44)	■ make it in time to (65) ■ more often than not (112) ■ not in this lifetime (84)

Travel	
■ have a journey (180) ■ have an adventure (180) ■ head (off) to (65, 108)	■ make one's way (somewhere) (78) ■ traffic congestion (118, 228) ■ trundle (7)

Work/Business	
■ be laid off (65) ■ capital (153) ■ corporate world (170) ■ declare all one's income (167) ■ economic prosperity (174) ■ established (153) ■ financial reserves (153) ■ forge a career (62) ■ have too many things on one's plate (128)	■ hedge fund (156) ■ high calibre (63) ■ merchandising (171) ■ peak of one's career (96) ■ public relations (174) ■ remuneration (174) ■ unfair labour practices (199) ■ work discrimination (199) ■ workaholic (199)

Cut-Up Study Notes

Part 1 Question + Position

Types	Questions	Positions
Ability	■ Can you...? ■ Are you able to...? ■ Are you capable of...? ■ Do you know how to...? ■ Are you good at...? ■ How good are you at...?	**Express your level of proficiency.** ■ I'm *an expert/a professional* at (V-ing or N). ■ I can (V) in my sleep. ■ I have a knack for (V-ing). ■ I'm a bit of a know-it-all when it comes to (V-ing or N). ■ I can't (V) to save my life. ■ I can't (V) for nuts. ■ I don't know the first thing about (V-ing or N).
Comparing	■ What are the (main) *differences/similarities* between ... and...? ■ How is ... *different from/similar to*...? ■ How are ... and ... alike?	**Identify the *differences/similarities*.** ■ They're like chalk and cheese. ■ ... bears no relation to... ■ There's a world of difference between ... and... ■ One of the major contrasts is... ■ The most striking resemblance is... ■ I can't tell them apart. ■ I can't draw a distinction between ... and...
Conditionals	■ What do you do if...? ■ What will you do if...? ■ What would you do if...? ■ What would you have done if...?	**State what you *will/would* do and substitute "if" with:** ■ As long as ■ Provided that ■ Say that ■ Unless ■ On condition that ■ Supposing that

Types	Questions	Positions
Describing	■ What is ... like? ■ How is...? ■ What does ... look like? ■ How do you...? ■ Can you describe...?	**State the most striking feature in an extreme way.** ■ (S) is *incredibly/terribly* (Adj). ■ (S) is an absolute (N). ■ (S) is one of the (superlative).
Negatives	■ What don't you *like/enjoy*...? ■ Is there anything you don't *like/enjoy*...? ■ Why don't you *like/enjoy*...?	**State what you dislike the most.** ■ I'm *sickened/disgusted* by... ■ I *despise/loathe/object to*... ■ (S) is a real turn-off. ■ I don't think much of...
Opinions	■ What do you think *about/of*...? ■ How do you feel about...?	**State a general opinion.** ■ In my opinion... ■ Personally, I feel... ■ I strongly believe... ■ I'm of the opinion that... ■ If you ask me... ■ To the best of my knowledge... ■ In my experience... ■ As far as I'm concerned... ■ As far as I know...
People	■ Who...? ■ Which person...? ■ What kind of people...?	**State who the person is.** ■ There's nobody like... ■ Nobody compares to... ■ Of all people, I'd have to say... ■ The one person who really (V) is... ■ I have a soft spot for... ■ I think the world of...

Types	Questions	Positions
Places	■ Where...? ■ Which place...? ■ What place...?	**State the name of the place.** ■ There's no place like... ■ Nowhere compares to... ■ Of all places, I'd have to say... ■ The one place which really (V) is... ■ My first choice is... ■ ... is as good a place as any.
Preferences	■ Do you prefer...? ■ Would you rather...? ■ Is it better to...? ■ Which is *better/more*...? ■ Is ... *better/more* (Adj) than...?	**Make a choice.** ■ Given the choice, I'd have to say... ■ If I had to take a pick, I'd *favour/go for*... ■ ... is no match for... ■ Give me ... any day.
Reasons	■ Why...? ■ What's the reason for...? ■ What's the cause of...? ■ What for...? ■ How come...?	**State the main reason.** ■ The reason (S) + (V) is... ■ The root of the problem is... ■ I'd put it down to the fact that... ■ ... plays a part in... ■ The only reason that comes to mind is... ■ Why in the world (S) + (V) is beyond me.
Suggestions	■ What should...? ■ What must...? ■ What do you recommend...? ■ What do you suggest...?	**State the strongest suggestion.** ■ I highly recommend... ■ If you want my advice, you ought to... ■ No matter what, you have to... ■ Take my advice and (V)... ■ You'd be well-advised to... ■ On no account should you... ■ I'd strongly advise against...

Types	Questions	Positions
Specifying	■ What kind of...? ■ What type of...? ■ What sort of...?	**Indicate which one in particular.** ■ There are a number of (N) but I would particularly like to mention... ■ There *is/are* a wide variety of (N) but I'd like to *single/point* out...
Superlatives	■ What's the most...? ■ What's the best...? ■ What's your favourite...? ■ What ... do you ... best?	**State what ranks the highest.** ■ ... takes the cake. ■ The pick of the bunch would have to be... ■ Nothing compares to... ■ ... is head and shoulders above the rest. ■ You can't beat ... for (reason). ■ ... runs rings around the others. ■ ... is streets ahead of the rest. ■ ... puts the rest to shame.
Time	■ How often...? ■ How many times...?	**State the frequency.** ■ I've never been known to (V). ■ Once in a blue moon, I... ■ I (V) *on and off/now and again/every so often/from time to time/every once in a while/whenever I get the chance.* ■ I have (PP) ... hundreds of times.
	■ When...? ■ What time...?	**State a specific time.** ■ There's no such time as... ■ Of all the times, I'd have to say... ■ The one time I really (V) is...

Types	Questions	Positions
Time	■ How much time...? ■ How long...?	**State the duration.** ■ *Longer/More* time than you can imagine. ■ I've spent *days/weeks/months/years/a lifetime.* ■ I spent a greater part of (time period) + (V-ing).
Yes/No	■ Do you...? ■ Are you...? ■ Will you...? ■ Have you...? ■ Are there...? ■ Did you...?	**Say yes or no in a different way.** ■ For "yes": definitely, for sure, without a doubt, naturally, of course, indeed, certainly, I'm afraid so ■ For "no": not at all, no way, not for the life of me, not a hope in hell, I'm afraid not, certainly not, not really, of course not, you must be kidding

Part 1, 2, 3 Support

Strategies	Examples of How to Begin
State a reason	■ The reason why (S) + (V) is... ■ A reason for this is... ■ It stands to reason that (N or V-ing) is... ■ The reason behind this is... ■ The *chief/most* compelling reason is... ■ The most obvious explanation is... ■ I'd put it down to... ■ I'd attribute it to... ■ It's all thanks to...
Give a result	■ As a result... ■ A direct result of (cause) is (effect). ■ The implications of (cause) is (effect). ■ At the end of the day (S) + (V). ■ The end result is that (S) + (V). ■ (effect) is the *product/result* of (cause). ■ (effect) *arises/stems/comes* from (cause).
Provide an example	■ A *classic/prime/fine/typical* example of this is... ■ ... is a *classic/prime/fine/typical* example of this. ■ Take ... for example. ■ There is no better example than... ■ In one case... ■ In some instances... ■ A case in point is... ■ ... to name but a few (used when giving many examples)
Contrast	■ Then again ■ All the same ■ Even so ■ On the other hand ■ *Although/Even though* ■ *While/Whereas* ■ In contrast to this... ■ Alternatively ■ *Despite/In spite of...* ■ Having said that...

Strategies	Examples of How to Begin
Explain a point more clearly	■ By this I mean... ■ What I'm trying to say is... ■ That is to say... ■ What I mean is... ■ In other words... ■ The thing is... ■ To put it another way... ■ Let me *explain/rephrase* that... ■ Put it this way... ■ All I'm saying is...
Add details	■ Besides... ■ What's more... ■ By the way... ■ And another thing... ■ ... not to mention (the fact that)... ■ On top of all this... ■ It's also worth mentioning...
Make a comparison	■ When comparing ... and... ■ If you compare ... and... ■ *In/By* comparison... ■ Comparatively speaking... ■ The more (S) + (V), the more (S) + (V). ■ (S) is *getting more and more/becoming increasingly*...
Discuss the benefits	■ The good thing about this is... ■ The major advantage is... ■ One of the *strengths/merits* is... ■ On the plus side... ■ The beauty of this is... ■ One of the added benefits is...

Strategies	Examples of How to Begin
Mention the drawbacks	■ The bad thing about this is... ■ The main disadvantage is... ■ One of the *weaknesses/shortcomings* is... ■ On the downside...
Touch on personal experiences	■ In my experience... ■ Speaking from experience... ■ One of my most *unforgettable/memorable/harrowing* experiences was... ■ From *bitter/personal* experience... ■ If I remember rightly... ■ I *distinctly/vividly/vaguely* remember a time... ■ I'll never forget... ■ The time I ... is still fresh in my mind. ■ I remember the time I ... as if it were yesterday.
Summarise	■ In a nutshell... ■ To cut a long story short... ■ All in all... ■ On the whole... ■ All things considered... ■ Generally speaking...

Part 3 Question + Position

Types of Questions	Examples	How to Answer
Predicting	■ How will ... *change/develop* in the next few decades? ■ Do you think ... will be different in 50 years time? ■ Could you *speculate/predict* what ... will be like 10 years from now?	**State the certainty of the event you suggest.** ■ In all probability... ■ There's every possibility that... ■ It's more than likely that... ■ There's *little/no* chance of (N) + (V-ing). ■ There's a *remote/slight* prospect of (N) + (V-ing).
Past Development	■ How was ... different 50 years ago? ■ Do you think ... *has/have* changed much since your *parents/ grandparents* were young? ■ Could you *describe/evaluate* how ... *has/have* developed over the past few decades?	**State how different it was.** ■ It's a whole new ball game these days. ■ ... nowadays bears no relation to the past. ■ ... these days is worlds apart from the past. ■ It was a radically different world (state time). ■ It was *considerably/significantly/ refreshingly/strikingly* different (state time). ■ Today's ... is a far cry from the past. ■ It was *slightly/subtly* different (state time).
Causes of Problems	■ Why do you think...? ■ What is the cause of...? ■ What is the reason for...? ■ Could you explain why...? ■ What explanations could you provide for...? ■ Could you justify...?	**State the main reason.** ■ The reason (S) + (V) is... ■ The only reason that comes to mind is... ■ The root of the problem is... ■ I'd put it down to... ■ ... plays a part in... ■ Why in the world (S) + (V) is beyond me.

Types of Questions	Examples	How to Answer
Results	■ What are the effects of...? ■ How does ... affect...? ■ What *influence/effect* does ... have on...? ■ What does ... lead to? ■ What does ... result in?	**State the main result.** ■ There are a number of *outcomes/ results/consequences/ after-effects/implications*, the main one being... ■ The main impact of ... is... ■ It has a far reaching effect on...
Solutions/ Suggestions	■ How could the problem of ... be solved? ■ What can be done about...? ■ What could the *government/ authorities* do to improve...? ■ Could you suggest some ways to make ... better?	**State the strongest suggestion.** ■ I'd put it before the authorities to... ■ They may as well... ■ I highly recommend... ■ If you want my advice, they ought to... ■ On no account should they... ■ No matter what, they have to... ■ Take my advice and (V). ■ They'd be well-advised to... ■ I'd strongly advise against...
Advantages/ Disadvantages	■ What are the advantages and disadvantages of...? ■ What are the benefits and drawbacks of...? ■ What are the pros and cons of...? ■ What are the merits and shortcomings of...? ■ What are the strengths and weaknesses of...? ■ What are the arguments for and against...? ■ What are the positive and negative sides of...? ■ What are the pluses and minuses of...?	**State the main *advantage/ disadvantage*.** ■ The *advantages/benefits/pros/ merits/strengths/positive sides/ pluses* are... ■ The beauty of ... is... ■ What makes ... so good is... ■ On the downside/upside... ■ Having said that, the *disandvantages/drawbacks/cons/ shortcomings/weaknesses/negative sides/minuses* are...

Types of Questions	Examples	How to Answer
Comparing	■ Could you compare the similarities and differences between...? ■ Could you *assess/evaluate* how ... and ... is *different/similar*? ■ Could you examine the main differences between ... and...?	**Identify the *differences/similarities*.** ■ One of the major contrasts is... ■ They're like chalk and cheese. ■ ... bears no relation to... ■ There's a world of difference between ... and... ■ The most striking resemblance is... ■ I can't tell them apart. ■ I can't draw a distinction between ... and...
Agree/Disagree	■ *Do/Would* you agree that...? ■ Do you think that...?	**State a general opinion.** ■ In my opinion... ■ Personally, I feel... ■ I strongly believe... ■ I'm of the opinion that... ■ If you ask me... ■ To the best of my knowledge... ■ In my experience... ■ As far as I'm concerned... ■ As far as I know... ■ To my mind...

Types of Questions	Examples	How to Answer
Identifying	■ What significance does ... have? ■ What dangers are there in...? ■ What right does ... have? ■ What responsibilities does ... have? ■ What effect does ... have? ■ What role does ... have? ■ Could you *outline/identify* the...?	**State the number and the main thing(s).** ■ There are a number of ... but I'd like to point out... ■ There are some ... but I'd like to single out... ■ There aren't many ... but I guess I could highlight... ■ The *key/main/major/prime/chief* + (N) is...
How + adj.	■ How important is...? ■ How much influence does ... have? ■ How effective is...? ■ How serious is the problem of...? ■ How *concerned/worried* are you about...? ■ How noticeable is the problem of...?	**State the degree with an adverb of intensity.** ■ *Highly/deeply/incredibly/unbelievably/remarkably/exceptionally/awfully/terribly/dreadfully* ■ *Fairly/pretty/quite/moderately/rather/somewhat/reasonably*

新东方大愚IELTS系列精品图书推荐

新东方独家引进

《剑桥雅思考试全真试题集 9》
（含光盘 2 张）
剑桥大学考试委员会　编著

定价：110 元　开本：16开　页码：176页

《剑桥雅思考试全真试题集 8》
（含光盘 2 张）
剑桥大学考试委员会　编著

定价：110 元　开本：16开　页码：176页

《剑桥雅思考试全真试题集 7》
（含光盘 2 张）
剑桥大学考试委员会　编著

定价：110 元　开本：16开　页码：176页

《剑桥雅思考试全真试题集 6》
（含光盘 2 张）
剑桥大学考试委员会　编著

定价：110 元　开本：16开　页码：176页

《剑桥雅思考试全真试题集 5》
（含光盘 2 张）
剑桥大学考试委员会　编著

定价：110元　开本：16开　页码：176页

◎ 4套完整的学术类雅思全真试题
◎ 2套培训类雅思阅读与写作全真试题

《剑桥雅思真题精讲 9》
周成刚　主编

定价：28元　开本：16开　页码：232页

《剑桥雅思真题精讲 8》
周成刚　主编

定价：28元　开本：16开　页码：208页

《剑桥雅思考试全真试题集 7 精讲》
周成刚　主编

定价：28 元　开本：16开　页码：234页

《剑桥雅思真题精讲 4、5、6》
周成刚　主编

定价：55元　开本：16开　页码：500页

◎ 洞悉雅思出题规律，精确剖析雅思真题
◎ 针对中国雅思考生的特点和需求，分题型全面破解

《剑桥雅思常见错误透析》
Pauline Cullen，Julie Moore　编著

定价：18元　开本：32开　页码：136页

《剑桥雅思语法》（附 MP3）
Diana Hopkins，Pauline Cullen　编著

定价：45 元　开本：16开　页码：272页

◎ 雅思备考资料官方出版机构推出的权威雅思语法教程
◎ 剑桥资深语法专家为全球雅思考生量身定做

《剑桥雅思核心词汇精讲精练》
（附 MP3）Pauline Cullen　编著

◎ 错误警示：帮助考生避免常见错误
◎ 单元测试：协助考生检验自己的进步
◎ 试题练习：涵盖学术类、培训类阅读以及写作、听力测试内容

定价：40元　开本：16开　页码：180页

《剑桥雅思写作高分范文》（附 MP3）
刘巍巍 方林　编著

◎ 收集十年雅思写作题目，全部写作话题一网打尽
◎ 从雅思写作题目出发，全面提高考生写作能力

定价：38元　开本：16开　页码：248页

《剑桥雅思 12 周完全攻略——阅读》
耿耿 乐静 孙吉芯 梅晗　编著

定价：35元　开本：16开　页码：320页

《剑桥雅思 12 周完全攻略——听力》
（附 MP3）　王超伟　编著

定价：29.8元　开本：16开　页码：184页

《剑桥雅思 12 周完全攻略——口语》
（附 MP3）　孙涛 王冬　编著

定价：29元　开本：16开　页码：204页

◎ 针对中国雅思考生的学习特点，制定12周科学备考方案
◎ 覆盖雅思阅读、听力、口语考试核心话题，提供权威答案，帮助考生有的放矢地备考

请登录新东方图书网www.dogwood.com.cn浏览更多图书

《雅思词汇词根+联想记忆法（加强版）》
（附 MP3） 俞敏洪 编著

◎ 完整收录雅思常考词汇，大量真题例句
◎ “词根+联想”实用有趣，配有插图，加深记忆
◎ 按字母顺序编排，增加返记菜单，便于考生进行自测

定价：58元 开本：16开 页码：528页

《雅思词汇词根+联想记忆法（乱序版）》
（附 MP3） 俞敏洪 编著

◎ 完整收录雅思常考词汇，大量真题例句
◎ “词根+联想”实用有趣，配有插图，加深记忆
◎ 增加返记菜单和索引，便于查找定位

定价：58元 开本：16开 页码：528页

《雅思词汇词根+联想记忆法》
（附 MP3） 俞敏洪 编著

◎ 原汁原味的真题例句，收词全面，涵盖雅思四大题型词汇
◎ 标出听力、口语单词，有针对性进行记忆

定价：32元 开本：32开 页码：368页

《雅思词汇词根+联想记忆法——写作》
俞敏洪 编著

定价：12元 开本：64开 页码：200页

《雅思词汇词根+联想记忆法——听力》
（附 MP3） 俞敏洪 编著

定价：12元 开本：64开 页码：160页

《雅思词汇词根+联想记忆法——口语》
（附 MP3） 俞敏洪 编著

定价：12元 开本：64开 页码：192页

《雅思词汇词根+联想记忆法——阅读》
（附 MP3） 俞敏洪 编著

定价：12元 开本：64开 页码：232页

◎ “词根+联想”实用有趣，配有插图，加深记忆
◎ 涵盖雅思阅读词汇，收词全面，分类科学

《雅思考官口语实战指导》
（附 MP3） **Mat Clark** 编著

◎ 分析中国考生的成绩现状，阐释评分系统的逐项要求
◎ 详尽介绍考试三部分程式，收录最新问题与话题卡片

定价：35元 开本：16开 页码：212页

《101雅思制胜法则：学术类》
（附 MP3）Garry Adams, Terry Peck 编著

定价：45元 开本：16开 页码：312页

《101雅思制胜法则：培训类》
（附 MP3）Garry Adams, Terry Peck 编著

定价：45元 开本：16开 页码：312页

《202 雅思技能强化训练》
（附 MP3）Garry Adams, Terry Peck 编著

定价：30元 开本：16开 页码：184页

《互动式三步搞定雅思 1001 词》
（附 CD-ROM） **Keith Burgess** 编著

定价：28元 开本：16开 页码：160页

《404雅思精编模考试题：学术类》
（附CD-ROM）
Donna Scovell, Vickie Pastellas, Max Knobel 编著

定价：34元 开本：16开 页码：224页

《404雅思精编模考试题：培训类》
（附CD-ROM）
Donna Scovell, Vickie Pastellas, Max Knobel 编著

定价：35元 开本：16开 页码：224页

这套教材由澳大利亚雅思培训专家编写，自出版以来受到全球考生的广泛赞誉，是备战雅思考试的必选材料。这套教材主要包含：《101雅思制胜法则》，分为学术类和培训类两册，内含101条实用雅思备考技巧及大量的模拟练习；《202雅思技能强化训练》，包含针对雅思题型而设置的202道英语技能练习题及拓展练习；《404雅思精编模考试题》，分为学术类和培训类两册，内含4套完整的雅思模考题及针对雅思考试各题型的备考建议；《互动式三步搞定雅思1001词》，帮助考生通过识记、转述、应用“三步走”轻松记忆雅思常考词。